W9-CJW-360

The Coming of the Lord

The Coming of the LORD

A Guide to the Sunday Readings
for Advent and the Christmas Season

J.D. CRICHTON

TWENTY-THIRD PUBLICATIONS
Mystic, Connecticut

242.33
C2C

North American Edition 1990

Twenty-Third Publications
185 Willow Street
P.O. Box 180
Mystic, CT 06355
(203) 536-2611

© 1990 J. D. Crichton. All rights reserved. No part of this publication may be reproduced in any manner without prior written permission of the publisher. Write to Permissions Editor.

ISBN 0-89622-461-9
Library of Congress Catalog Card Number 90-62565

Originally published in Great Britain by Kevin Mayhew, Ltd. (Rattlesden, Bury St. Edmunds, Suffolk 1P3O OSZ)

Preface

In this book I have given a summary history of the origins of Advent, the Christmas season and of the Feast of the Presentation of the Lord in the Temple. These essays have their importance as they throw light on how Christians of earlier centuries understood these feasts and seasons and help us to understand, at least in part, how the texts, scriptural and liturgical, came to be chosen.

After the seasons and feasts I have written specimen homilies which, as I said in my *Journey through Lent*, are intended to give pointers to what might be said. They are not intended to be preached as they stand. As the Constitution on the Sacred Liturgy says (no. 35/2), the preacher has to expound the Scriptures, and their message should be applied to the life of the people. The homilist speaks to the people in front of him and tries to meet their needs and aspirations. But his sources, says the Constitution, are the Scriptures and the liturgical texts. The latter are often overlooked yet they often give a clue to the basic message of the Scriptures in their liturgical context.

Another problem occurs when the infancy gospels, which form the substance of the Scripture readings for the Christmas season are read too literally. They need to be treated carefully. According to the best exegetes, they are not to be regarded as quasi-photographic records of the events of the birth of Christ and all that followed from it. Both Matthew and Luke were concerned to show that Jesus was the Son of God, whose coming fulfilled the ancient prophecies. It is inappropriate to use small details of these accounts, the more picturesque and colorful ones, on which to base a homily. The tremendous statements of Matthew about the Emmanuel and of St. Luke about the holy child who will be the Son of God give us food for thought for many a long day and, however they are presented, they are the heart of the Christmas message.

The Feast of the Presentation, which has a complicated history, is the epilogue to the Christmas season and is best seen in that light.

J.D.C.

Contents

The Coming of the Lord

1

The Origins of Advent

The First Christian feast was the celebration of the Paschal Mystery on the first day of the week, the Lord's Day or Sunday. By the second century this had become an annual celebration with a fast from the preceding Friday until the early hours of Easter Sunday. Under the impact of the catechumenate and the discipline of penance, Lent developed into a six-week period.[1] It was not, however, until the middle of the fourth century that the anniversary of the birth of Christ came to be celebrated. It is first recorded in a calendar of 336/354 A.D. and the commemoration may have been kept even a little earlier. In Rome there was no Advent. In Spain, however, toward the end of the century in the year 380, people were exhorted to attend church more frequently for a period of three weeks from December 17 to the Epiphany though this was a time for *baptism* which there and at that time often took place on the Feast of the Epiphany. Since baptism was in question, fasting and more frequent prayer were elements in the preparation. The association of baptism with the Epiphany suggests influence from the Eastern church. In Gaul (France) from the feast of St. Martin, November 11, the people were urged to fast on three days of the week until Christmas. The ascetical element of Advent was thus marked in the practice of these two churches, but it is not possible to say that it influenced later developments. Nor, for want of evidence, can we find any eschatological dimension at this time. In both cases Advent was oriented to Christmas and in Spain to Christmas-Epiphany.

In Rome the season of Advent, first six weeks and then four, makes its appearance for the first time in the sixth century. It seems to have had some difficulty in making its way into the liturgical year. In the sacramentaries (early missals) the texts are not included in the Proper of Time but are placed after the Proper of Saints. It was not until the eighth or ninth centuries and even later that the liturgical books inserted the Masses of Advent in the Proper of Time.

More important than the dates and facts is the meaning of Advent. For Rome, and Ravenna in the north of Italy, Advent was a period of preparation for the first coming of Christ, though that did not entirely exclude the eschatological theme, the second coming of the Lord at the end of time. This is apparent in one or two prayers of the sixth-century Gelasian Sacramentary: "Lord, rouse up your power and come. What you have promised your church *at the end of time*, in your mercy make effective within us now." Another prayer, of which we still use a revised version on Christmas Eve, delivers a similar message: "Almighty God, grant that *the solemnity of our redemption* we are about to celebrate may bring us help in this life and give us *the rewards of everlasting happiness*."

These prayers are enlightening in two ways. The first links the "then" and the "now." The church prays that the power the Son of God will exert at the end of time to bring his redeeming work to final completion will be available to the Christian community as it prepares for the coming of Christ at Christmas. In this perspective there are three comings: at the incarnation, at the end of time, and "in sacrament," that is in and through the Christmas liturgy. All are linked to one another and are so celebrated during Advent and Christmas. The second prayer looks immediately to the feast of Christmas. St. Leo the Great (d. 461) in his Christmas sermons sees it as the beginning of "the solemnity of our redemption." But the prayer also looks to the end, when the victory over sin and death will be complete, and all who are faithful will enter into "everlasting happiness."

There is, however, another strand in the liturgy of Advent that from the early Middle Ages played a significant part in it. The second coming was thought of almost exclusively in the terms of the Last Judgment, which would be a time of terror when the whole human race would be gathered together and arraigned before God. Then secret sins would be revealed, the wicked sent to hell, and the righteous would enter into glory. This is something of an over-simplification of the New Testament data but perhaps understandable in the seventh century when Western civilization seemed to be in an advanced state of collapse. In Italy the Lombards were dominating the whole peninsula from the north, and St. Gregory the Great (d. 604) wrote of living *inter gladios Longobardorum* (between Lombard swords), and in more than one homily spoke in very gloomy terms of the end of the world, which he seems to have thought was coming soon. St. Columba, the austere Irish monk, who wrote some impolite letters to Gregory, was of the same mind. Later still, sculptors began to carve their "Dooms" on the tympans of great churches and cathedrals, and painters on the walls. Scenes of horror were depicted, corpses were shown struggling from their tombs, devils of fearsome aspect were forking people into hell, and perhaps some of the artists got a certain gruesome pleasure out of their work as they (cheerfully?) consigned popes and bishops and kings into hell. It was the mood of the *Dies irae*, the Day of Wrath and Bitterness, a hymn that was written for use in Advent in the thirteenth century.

It was this aspect of things that gave Advent its ascetical and penitential character. Hence the purple vestments and the days of fasting and abstinence on Wednesdays, Fridays and Saturdays, a discipline lasting into this century, turning Advent into a second Lent. But never complete, at least as far as the liturgy was concerned. The Alleluias remained, as they still do, and they are a trace of a more joyful expectation of the second coming. On the other hand, the Gloria was and is suppressed so that it can be sung with a new joy and solemnity at Christmas.

There are still, however, one or two difficulties about Advent. It is often thought of as the beginning of the liturgical year and chronologically, this seems to be so. But, as we have seen, the early sacramentaries seemed to be uncertain. If there was a beginning it was the feast of Christmas itself, regarded as the beginning of salvation. In this perspective Christmas looked to the celebration of the Paschal Mystery at Easter, and some modern scholars, setting aside the chronological scheme, have suggested that the celebration of the Paschal Mystery is the real beginning of the liturgical year because, both theologically and liturgically, all else flows out from it, back to Christmas and on to the time after Easter and indeed to the end of time.

Another difficulty is to see *when* Advent begins. The scriptural texts of the last two Sundays of the Year in all three cycles very clearly have for their theme the second coming of Christ and lap over the first part of Advent. Are these Sundays a sort of pre-Advent? In fact, the whole of the last part of the liturgical year is oriented to the Last Things. Even in the Proper of Saints we have the feast of All Saints which draws our minds to heaven, and the Commemoration of All Souls which, apart from being an occasion to pray for the dead, suggests to us thoughts of death and the afterlife. With the last Sundays of the Year and at least the First Sunday of Advent, the homilist has in fact an opportunity to use them as occasions to speak of the considerable material in the Old and New Testaments about the Day of the Lord in its many aspects.

Whether or not the liturgical year begins in Advent, according to the Roman Calendar (Chapter I, no. 2), Advent is a time of preparation for the second coming of Christ at the end of time and for his birth at Christmas. The second coming receives some emphasis in the first part of December, though the theme is not followed rigidly or even quite consistently. Both in the Divine Office and the Mass there are texts more concerned with Christmas than the second coming. But from December 17 to 24 the liturgy is wholly concerned with the first coming of Christ. In other words, there is a slight ambivalence about the season. The two comings are separated but in fact intersect and, as we have seen, one is connected with the other. It is this that gives a unity to the whole season.

It is against this background that we should understand the use the church makes of the Scriptures from both the Testaments. In Years A and B we have passages from Isaiah for the first readings and in Year C other prophets are used. Most of these texts look beyond the first coming to the Day of the Lord, which in the Old Testament was multi-faceted. Sometimes, as frequently in Isaiah, the text looks to the deliverance from the captivity of Babylon and the restoration of Israel, often described in very colorful and idealistic terms. At other times, the Day of the Lord is a time of terror and judgment, though this is not prominent in the Advent texts. On yet other occasions the texts foretell the coming of a Messiah, though the prophets were never able to say who the Messiah would be or when he would come. Here it is useful to remember what the experts call the "fuller sense" of holy Scripture. This is a sense that goes beyond anything that the prophets could envisage or intend. When Isaiah spoke of the son who would be born of the young girl, he may have been thinking of a son for Hezekiah, but scholars do not agree on the subject. It would seem that in later Old Testament times the Jews themselves saw someone more in the "son" than a royal child. The translators of the Septuagint, about 200 B.C., translated the Hebrew word for "young girl" as *parthenos*, the Greek for "virgin," and Matthew's gospel simply took this over. The Christian church, pondering on this and many other messianic texts, saw in the foretold Messiah, the Anointed one of God, Jesus who was born of the Virgin at Bethlehem. For the church, too, the Day of the Lord is both the day of the coming of the Christ and the final Day when he will appear in glory. So once again we see that the two comings are interlocked.

But the church makes use of the Old Testament for another reason. If we read especially some of the Isaian texts with care we find that the prophet is thinking of the return of the exiles from Babylon as a second exodus, and in this way and in others he is recalling God's dealing with the people of the Old Testament which we call the history of salvation. As we hear on II Advent (Year A) these things were written for "our encouragement," we renew our hope. For the Old Testament is not just a record of certain events as if they were mere history. They are the record of what God had done for his people throughout the centuries when he took the initiative. The all-holy God *approaches* the people, offering them his love which he sealed with the paschal sacrifice in the desert to make them his own people if they would respond to him with faith and obedience. One message of Advent is that what the "Redeemer of Israel" did then he will do now, and does do now if we respond with faith, obedience and love to his Word, for whose renewed coming to us we prepare during Lent.

Always and everywhere in Advent, and indeed in the season of Christmas, we are concerned with "coming," and that word, if we understand something of its origins, can lead us into a deeper understanding. In the world of the Roman Empire the Greek word *parousia* was closely associated with another word, *epiphaneia*, epiphany. Both were used for the coming-arrival of the emperor or his representative who came with all pomp and ceremony and who would perhaps confer status or privileges on the city he was visiting. The church adopted the term, and in the West it was translated *adventus*. It is thus used among other places in the Divine Office: "See, the Lord comes from afar. His splendor fills the whole world," and "The Son of God is coming with great power: All mankind shall see his face and be reborn," though that may refer to Christmas also. Then there is the great and ancient responsory: "I am watching from afar. I see the Lord coming with his might, and a cloud covering all the earth...." There are other texts like one from Isaiah 40:10: "See, the Lord comes with might," and the collect which prays that "when Christ comes again we may go out to meet him with the fruits of repentance and be gathered into the kingdom of heaven."[2] The sense of a glorious coming of the Lord is clear.

The theme of the parousia-epiphany, the arrival of the Lord, is found in the Christmas liturgy, too. Thus the entrance chant for the Night Mass is "The Lord said to me: You are my Son; today I have begotten you," but if the rest of the psalm were sung, as it once was, we should find: "It is I who have set up my king on Zion, my holy mountain." In the first reading from Isaiah 9, the child that is born for us is a prince, the Prince of Peace, but his dominion is wide and he established his royal power forever. In the Letter to Titus (Night Mass and Dawn Mass) we find the word "epiphany," both verb and noun. The birth of the child is the arrival of a great king, yet we are awaiting the full and final appearance of the Lord of glory. On the feast of Epiphany the church sings of Christ as Lord and King: "The Lord and ruler is coming; kingship is his, and government and power" (entrance chant), and the responsorial psalm puts before us a picture of the King who is both powerful and merciful.

The paradox of the Christian faith is that the Babe of Bethlehem is also King and Lord of the world. If these texts of the liturgy seem to strike a strange and even unwelcome note, it would be well to remember them. Christmas can dissolve into a welter of sentimentality and we are inclined to forget the might and majesty of God, whom we should reverence and worship. It is that same God "living in unapproachable light" who, out of his infinite love and generosity, has bent down to our lowly condition and has rescued us from sin and death so that he can raise us up to himself.

It has been said often enough, and St. Bernard said it long ago, that Advent-Christmas is concerned with three comings: Christ's coming at Christmas, his coming at the end of time, and his coming to us. The saying prompts the question: Is this first coming just a matter of remembering an event long past? And further, are we to look for the second coming of the Lord with no more than a vague apprehension? There is in fact a deeper meaning to the word "coming." The Lord and his Holy Spirit came to us in baptism and confirmation, and constantly in the eucharist we pray that we may "be nourished by the body and blood of Christ" and be filled by the Holy Spirit *so that* "we may become one body, one spirit in Christ." In Advent we pray: "God of power and mercy, open our hearts in welcome..." (I Advent), and, as the same prayer goes on, we ask that we may let nothing in our life and conduct hinder us from *"receiving* Christ with joy." During Advent, then, we try to open our hearts so that when Christ comes to us *in sacramento*, in and through the sacramental liturgy at Christmas, we may be ready to receive him. *Then* he renews his presence within us so that we can take up our life again and live more effectively for him, for the church and for others. It may well be that he is calling us to bear witness to him and his gospel in a new way. For the Christian life is not static but dynamic, and through our celebration of Advent and Christmas we are given a new grace-filled impetus. It is for us to welcome it and receive it unto ourselves. This in turn is a preparation, the best preparation, for the second coming. As the same prayer indicates, we pray that "when he comes in glory" we shall "become one with him."

Notes
1. See J.D. Crichton, *Journey through Lent.*
2. See I Advent, Office of Readings.

2

Liturgies of Advent

Year A

FIRST SUNDAY OF ADVENT

Isaiah 2:1–5
Psalm 121
Romans 13:11–14
Matthew 24:37–44

The keynote of the liturgy today is one of expectancy. Isaiah's vision goes far beyond the immediate future. The glorious Temple of Solomon was still standing in Jerusalem but there will be a new Temple to which all the nations of the world will stream, there to be taught by God how they should behave, keep his law, and do his will. He seems to be envisaging an entirely new age when peace will reign, when the peoples of the world will "hammer their swords into ploughshares and their spears into sickles," and there will be no more war. In other words, he is speaking of the end-time when the whole redeeming work of God will be brought to completion and all peoples will "walk in the light of the Lord."

Whether or not he thought such a world would in fact come about on this earth we cannot say. But the place of this passage on the First Sunday of Advent suggests to us a messianic sense. The new Temple of the Lord where all will learn his ways is in this perspective the church, the body of Christ (cf. John 2:22), where the word of God will be proclaimed and offered to all who will listen to it. Then indeed there will be a peace that "surpasses understanding," when in his Son the whole world is reconciled, for as the prophet Micah declared, "He himself will be peace" (5:4).[1]

The gospel of today, however, is concerned with the Day of the Lord, the end-time. It is part of a long chapter in which we can discern two levels of meaning. Much of the passage is envisaging the destruction of Jerusalem that took place in 70 A.D., and the evangelists saw this as a foreshadowing of the end when this world will undergo a transformation and there will be "a new heaven and a new earth." Then the Lord will appear in glory, his work of salvation will be completed, and there will be the final revelation of God and his loving purpose to draw all to himself, a purpose he has been working out through, and often in spite of, the sins and crimes and brutalities that have marked human history. Then Jesus will appear as "King of kings and Lord of lords," and all the hosts of heaven will sing, "Alleluia! Victory and glory and power to our God. He judges fairly and punishes justly..." (Revelation 19:16, 2). This is a picture of the final glory of Jesus Christ, and this is why the New Testament and, so often, the liturgy can invite us to "await in joyful hope the coming of our Savior, Jesus Christ." Indeed, as we learn from the Book of Revelation, it was the expectation of this glorious consummation that sustained the hope of the Christians of the first century.

The message of the day then is a simple one. It is for the second coming of the Lord that we must prepare. Recalling the ancient story of Noah, Jesus suggests that the people *were* warned but took no notice. They went on eating and drinking and taking wives and husbands up to the day the flood came and swept them all away. The second coming will be equally sudden and no one knows when it will be, not even the Son of Man, and its effects could be equally catastrophic if people do not prepare. That is why we must "stay awake," be on the alert, like the prudent householder who takes the necessary precautions against burglary.

How are we to do that? First, we must listen to the word of God that comes to us from the Scriptures. Again and again they warn us to remember that this life must come to an end, both our own and that of the whole universe. And that is not an easy lesson to learn. Most of us are tempted to think we are immortal and that this world will go on forever. Eating, drinking, marrying, earning a living, and perhaps having a good time are in the forefront of our concerns. But they, too, will and must come to an end. And what then? That is a question the Advent liturgy poses to us and that is the message we must attend to today.

Next, St. Paul, with the second coming very much in mind, tells us that we must change our lives, and he lists some of the more lurid vices: drunkenness, promiscuity, licentiousness—which seem to be prevalent in our society today—but also wrangling and jealousy. If that seems rather negative, let us remember that immediately before this passage comes the verse, "You must love your neighbor as yourself." If you do that you will be "fulfilling the law," and will do no harm to anyone, including yourself. This, fundamentally, is the "armor of the Lord Jesus Christ." The love he inserts into our hearts by his Holy Spirit is the power enabling us to resist all sin and to serve others as he did. This sentiment is echoed in the Prayer over the Offerings: "As we serve you now, accept our offering and sustain us with your promise of eternal life." Indeed, in the Eucharist we celebrate there is more than a promise. There is a pledge, a guarantee: "Anyone who eats my flesh and drinks my blood *has* eternal life" (John 6:54).

Second Sunday of Advent

Isaiah 11:1–10
Psalm 71
Romans 15:4–9
Matthew 3:1–12

The people of the ancient world looked back to an earthly paradise that they thought had once existed, and the human race as a whole seems to have a longing for a future when there will be a world of harmony, justice, and peace. Perhaps it may even be an obscure longing for God which is rooted in our hearts. Advent looks back to the past: "everything that was written in the Scriptures was written to teach us." We are to learn from the example of the patriarchs and prophets who through all the twists and turns of their tragic history remained faithful to God and proclaimed his message. But Advent also looks to the future, and this may give us a clue to the extraordinary prophecy of Isaiah who speaks of the wolf living with the lamb, the calf and the lion feeding together, and the rest. Advent is about two comings, the coming of the Lord in glory at the end of time and the coming of the Son of God as a man in Bethlehem. We shall find that the two are interlocked.

Isaiah takes us back to the past, a distant past, though he was looking to the future. "A shoot will spring from Jesse"; the prophet is reminding us and the people who heard him of the promise of a Messiah. He will come from the family of Jesse, from David in whom God had vested the messianic promise which is proclaimed, among other places, in Psalm 131: "The Lord swore an oath to David; A son, the fruit of your body, will I set upon your throne." On this descendant of David, says Isaiah, the Spirit of the Lord will rest and in him will be found the Spirit that gave gifts of wisdom and knowledge, the Spirit that inspired the prophets to proclaim that one day in an unknown future a Messiah would come. He will be like a king, the sort of king of whom we sing in today's Psalm: "He will judge the people in justice, he will listen to the cry of the poor"; he will have pity for them and save them from oppression. He will be the messianic King who combines power with mercy and love.

It is this Messiah that John the Baptist discerns and proclaims. He is greater than John who is not worthy to untie the strap of his sandals. He is bringing in an entirely new order. He will bring a new and a different kind of baptism. He will send the Holy Spirit, the Spirit who separates the wheat from the chaff, the Spirit who inspires repentance in the human heart. That is why John could cry out, "Repent, the kingdom of heaven is near."

But what is that kingdom of heaven? Like other writers of the Old Testament, Isaiah seems to envisage a new age which will be a kind of paradise where the wolf will live in peace with the lamb, and the calf and the lion cub feed together. He seems to have been thinking of an earthly paradise when there would be an unparalleled era of prosperity and peace. As he imagined it, it has never come about, and Jesus had to refine all this and tell the people that the Day of the Lord will usher in an entirely new order of things. The Messiah is no earthly king and his Kingdom will be no earthly kingdom. All who come to him by faith and are united to him by baptism and the eucharist will be taken up by him into the new heaven where in indescribable joy they will see God face to face.

Advent is a time of preparation for our meeting with the Lord at the end of our lives and at the end of time. It prepares us also for the coming of Christ within us at Christmas and this itself is a preparation for the second coming. As we sing in the Advent hymn:

Lo! The Lamb so long expected,
Comes with pardon down from heaven;
Let us haste with tears of sorrow,
One and all to be forgiven.

So when next he comes in glory,
Shrouding all the earth in fear,
May he then as our defender
On the clouds of heaven appear.

The Scriptures today suggest two ways of preparing. We must listen to the word of God, taking its message to our hearts and living by it: "Everything that was written long ago in the Scriptures was meant to teach us...." If we do, it leads us on to repentance in response to John's call, "Repent, the kingdom of heaven is near." That repentance, the turning of our minds and hearts to God, will be deepened and made effective if we take part in a service of penitence when through the sacrament Jesus communicates to us his eternal love and mercy.

THIRD SUNDAY OF ADVENT

Isaiah 35:1–6a, 10
Psalm 145
James 5:7–10
Matthew 11:2–11

Whenever we hear that passage from Isaiah I imagine that we cannot fail to be moved by it. Here is the God of love and mercy. Through his prophet he is giving his people in captivity a message of hope and comfort. There will be a new exodus, they will be restored to their land and the land itself will flourish as it had done before. On their journey back, the Lord will strengthen weary hands carrying burdens, the trembling knees tired by the long pilgrimage, and all will be borne up by the message, "Courage; do not be afraid."

The prophecy was fulfilled but only partially. The people did return but they found that they had to rebuild almost everything and in the most difficult circumstances. As they painfully rebuilt the Temple, they had to do so with the trowel in one hand and the sword in the other.

Then, as we read on, we ask ourselves: "Were the eyes of the blind opened, the ears of the deaf unsealed, were dumb tongues loosened, and lame able to walk?" The answer is, "No, not yet." Like other prophets, Isaiah's vision went beyond the more immediate future even if he did not know what that future would be. He had already sketched out a portrait of the Messiah (9:5–6; 11:1–9), but he did not know who he would be or when he would come.

We learn that only from the gospel. John the Baptist, now in Herod's prison, had heard of what the Messiah was doing and either he or his followers were wondering whether this Jesus was the Messiah whom the prophets had promised would come. Perhaps, like even the disciples of Jesus, they thought that he would be an earthly king who would come with great power and majesty. So John's followers come to Jesus to question him and for reply he quotes Isaiah: the blind are seeing, the lame walking, lepers are being cleansed, the deaf have their hearing restored, and (what Isaiah had never spoken of) even the dead are raised to life. These works of mercy were indeed signs that Jesus was the One who was to come. John's disciples could now go back and report to John what was happening. They and John, who knew their Old Testament as well as anyone, could now realize that Jesus was indeed the promised Messiah. He had come, he was here, and at least some of John's disciples would henceforth follow Jesus.

Isaiah had foretold the coming of a Messiah but his arrival did not mean the end. It was not more than the end of an era and the beginning of a new one. By his life, work, and teaching Jesus proclaimed the Kingdom. The prophets all led up to John, the last of the prophets, but now a new age was beginning, the messianic age (cf. Matthew 11:13). It is the age of the Kingdom, and, as so many of the parables indicate, it is dynamic. It is a growing thing, like the mustard seed or the yeast in the dough. And of that Kingdom the church is the beginning, for the messianic age is also the age of the church. Throughout that age there has been a partial fulfillment of Isaiah's prophecy. The signs of divine power have continued, the blind have had their sight restored to them, the sick and the lame have been healed, and, what is more, the Good News of salvation has been proclaimed throughout the world. But, as we are well aware, there are still many millions who have not heard the gospel, and their numbers are steadily increasing in Western industrialized societies. There are yet other millions who are poor and oppressed, and all these must be the active concern of the inhabitants of the Kingdom. For the Kingdom is not just the church. We have the word of Vatican II that the whole created universe is also of the Kingdom. All sound human effort is gradually building up the Kingdom. Nothing is excluded. If countless numbers of the sick, the blind, the deaf, and the lame have been healed in our own time through modern medicine, that, too, is part of the ongoing process, part of God's work mediated through human beings.

The saving and healing work must go on, for even the messianic age is not the final end. It is reaching on to that final consummation when the work of salvation will be completed and the

Lord-Messiah will appear in glory and all those who have worked along with him, even unknowingly, will be carried over into the eternal Kingdom of his marvelous light.

Meanwhile, says St. James, we must have patience: "Think of the farmer; how patiently he waits for the precious fruit of the ground until it has had the autumn rains and the spring rains! You too have to be patient; do not lose heart, because the Lord's coming will be soon." James did not know, nor do we, when that "soon" will be. As for us, we need to be patient, patient with others but also with ourselves. We cannot be spiritually "perfect" all at once. That will only be achieved when at the end of our lives "the love of God will be brought to perfection in us" (1 John 4:12), in the measure that God has destined for us. And, if I may say so, we need, like the farmer, to be patient with God. We cannot always understand his ways. There are insoluble mysteries in our experience and in the experience of the whole human race. But God is always faithful to his people, he never abandons us, he is in control, and all through the events of history he is working out his saving plan for us and for the whole human race. That is what will be revealed to us when the kingdom is brought to its final perfection and we shall see the glory, the goodness, and the unfailing love of the Lord.

FOURTH SUNDAY OF ADVENT

Isaiah 7:10–14
Psalm 23
Romans 1:1–7
Matthew 1:18–24

We are very familiar with the gospel story of today. We have known it since our early childhood. And often enough we have heard the prophecy of Isaiah about the maiden who would conceive and give birth to a son. But this very familiarity may dull our understanding of the wonder of the event that the Scriptures describe. We may deepen our understanding with a few minutes of reflection.

Isaiah was speaking at a time when Jerusalem was being besieged by a powerful army. If the city fell and the king was captured and perhaps put to death, the succession of the royal house of David would be in danger. The prophet, moved by God, wanted to give Ahaz reassurance that the city would not fall and that there would be a son to succeed him. For some reason the king rejected the sign offered him but, nevertheless, Isaiah in very solemn fashion foretells the birth of a son. He remembered that God had promised that a Messiah would come from the house of David, and God is faithful to his promises. He would not fail Ahaz or his people in their hour of need. Whether the birth of a son to Ahaz or any future descendant would exhaust the promise he could hardly know.

But the people did not forget the promise. They and their learned men pondered it through the centuries and when, about 200 B.C., the Jewish scholars translated the Hebrew Old Testament into Greek, for the Hebrew word for "maiden" they put *parthenos*, "virgin." When Matthew was giving his account of the conception of Jesus he, too, remembered the text: "The virgin will conceive and give birth to a son."

Matthew's account is simple and straightforward but that word "Emmanuel," which he also took over from Isaiah, gives us pause. As we ponder that word we become aware, with the evangelists, that we are in the presence of a stupendous event. The all-holy, the almighty God, the God who is total love, has shared his love with us in giving us his Son: "God so *loved* the world as to give his only Son that all who believe in him might not be lost but have eternal life." He is Jesus, the One who is to save the people from their sins. At the same time, he is the all-holy, all-loving Son who did not cling to his equality with the Father but lowered himself, taking on our sinful condition. He is Emmanuel who came to live among us, as he still does, making his love present to us, and through word and sacrament making himself available to us. He is the "Word who was made flesh and lived among us."

Yet stupendous as this event is, it came about in the stillness of a cottage in Nazareth where Mary heard the message, "The Holy Spirit will come upon you and the power of the Most High will overshadow you and the child will be holy and will be called the Son of God." The accounts of Matthew and Luke are very different in literary form but they deliver exactly the same message.

Sometimes God seems very far away, but as we reflect on these texts we become aware of the tremendous truth that God is with us. We understand something of the overwhelming love of God sweeping out from his heart to every human creature to rescue them from the alienation of sin and wretchedness, and to unite them to himself, to his love. Indeed, with St. John we can see "God, made visible in Jesus Christ": "What existed from the beginning, what we have heard and what we have seen with our own eyes, the Word who is life—that is our subject" (1 John 1:1). Not that we see him as the disciple did or hear his voice. But we hear his word in the Scriptures and we "see" him, perceive him, in the sacraments which are the manifestation of Emmanuel, God who is with us.

But of course we cannot hope to grasp the full depth and breadth of the love of God that is so near to us and indeed in us, but with the English saint, the Venerable Bede, we might like to make his reflections our own in the busy days that lie ahead.

Commenting on the Magnificat, he puts these words on her lips:

The Lord has exalted me with a great and unheard of gift, which cannot be explained in any words and can be scarcely understood by the deepest feelings of the heart. And so I offer up all the strength of my soul in thanksgiving and praise. In my joy I pour out all my life, all my feeling, all my understanding in contemplating the greatness of him who is without end. My spirit rejoices in the eternal divinity of Jesus my Savior, whom I conceived in time and bear in my body.[2]

Notes

1. Micah 4:1-3 is related to the Isaian passage fo this day.
2. *Divine Office* I, 22 December, p. 156.

3

Liturgies of Advent

Year B

FIRST SUNDAY OF ADVENT

Isaiah 63:16b–17, 19b; 64:2b–7
Psalm 79
1 Corinthians 1:3–9
Mark 13:33–37

Advent of Years B and C follow the same pattern as Year A: The first Sunday is about the Last Day of the Lord, the next two are about John the Baptist, and the fourth is centered upon Our Lady. The themes are thus the same, and it is difficult for the homilist to avoid repetition. It would seem best to "search the Scriptures" as they are laid out before us each Sunday.

In the gospel today we hear the external message of Advent: "Be on your guard, stay awake, because you never know when the time will come." It would seem, however, that we should give particular attention to the reading from Isaiah. He has something important to say to us about "waiting for the Lord."

The prophet is uttering a long prayer of supplication of which our passage is but a section. He is expressing the sentiments of the people now in exile in Babylon. Their land has been devastated by the enemy, the holy Temple where God made himself known to them is no more, and they are aliens in a pagan and perhaps hostile country. On their behalf the prophet acknowledges that their Lord is their Father and that they are totally dependent on him. Though Father, he is the potter and they the clay which he formed with his hands (Genesis 2:7). Yet they have gone astray after false gods; they have forgotten how to reverence the all-holy God in true worship that took place in the Temple. Now they are reaping what they have sown. They are sinners, like withered leaves blown about by the wind. God seems to have turned his face away from them.

Then in the middle of the prayer comes the great cry, "Oh, that you would tear the heavens open and come down." We may regard this as simply a cry for rescue by a mighty act of God. But it is more than that. It is a prayer that the people may once more be aware that God is with them. In a wider perspective it is the expression of the ineradicable longing of the human heart for God. Throughout the ages human beings have sought God, often in the most bizarre forms, through images made by human hands, through strange and sometimes immoral rites, through superstitions and magic, which is an attempt to use God for our own purposes. This is not just a matter of past history. One of the most disturbing features of the age we live in is that people no longer seem to have any desire for God. They are in pursuit of idols like money, unnecessary possessions, and what they regard as the Good Life which so often is the Bad Life. And it may be that because of the stifling of the desire for God some are resorting to Satanism and various forms of magic. It is to be hoped that one day, like the people of Israel, they will confess that they have sinned and then the desire for God will be revived in them.

Again the prophet voiced the desire of the people: "No ear has heard, no eye has seen any god act as you do for those who trust him." If the prophet was interpreting the desires of the exiles correctly, perhaps he was suggesting that they were looking for an intervention of God like his rescue of the people from Egypt or his vivid appearance on Mount Sinai when he made his presence known to them. The prophet himself may have been looking on the Day of the Lord though he could not know what would then be revealed. This would only be made known in the New Testament, as St. Paul very well realized. Jesus Christ was the fulfillment of all that had been promised throughout the ages. St. Paul proclaims Jesus as the wisdom of God and, seizing on and adapting the sentence of the prophet, he asserts that Jesus is the wisdom of God revealed in the world which none of the masters of this age have ever known. It is he who will lead people to the vision of God: "We teach what Scripture calls the thing that no eye has seen and no ear heard, things beyond the mind of man, all that God has prepared for those who love him" (1 Corinthians 2:8–9). The One who had been desired and awaited so long had come and through him humanity would eventually be able to see what the human mind cannot conceive, all that God has to offer to those who love him—to those who, seeking, would find him and in finding him would have complete fulfillment and lasting joy. That is the promise.

We meanwhile must "stay awake," we must keep vigil, and vigil implies prayer, remaining open to God even in the midst of our daily and necessary tasks. And part of our prayer at this time should be that we shall never lose the desire for God, a desire that is sustained and nourished by the Holy Eucharist we now celebrate. Thus prepared, we can "wait in *joyful* hope for the coming of our Savior Jesus Christ."

SECOND SUNDAY OF ADVENT

Isaiah 40:1-5, 9–11
Psalm 84
2 Peter 3:8–14
Mark 1:1–18

Today there is strong contrast between the first reading and the gospel. Through his prophet God is announcing the return of the people to their homeland. A voice cries, "Prepare in the wilderness a way for the Lord. Make a straight highway for our God...Let every valley be filled in...," and so on. The prophet was thinking of a royal progress, when in the ancient world it was customary to level the hilly roads and fill up hollow places. It was what was later called a *parousia* and the king's arrival an *epiphany*, the appearance of an almost divine person in all his glory who deigns to come among his people.

Then there is the Voice of the gospel that we immediately identify with John the Baptist who, though "a messenger of God," is nothing like a royal herald. He has lived in the wilderness; he is a prophet wearing the clothes of a prophet and like the prophets eating what he could find in the desert. In mysterious terms he announces One who is to come after him but that one does not appear as a king. He arrives among the sinners and, as if he were one of them, he seeks baptism from John. He is expressing his solidarity with those he had come to save. That perhaps, more than anything else, points up the contrast between the prophet's message and the One who is now proclaimed. He is totally unlike an oriental king. As Matthew wrote, borrowing another passage from the prophet, "He will not break the crushed reed, nor put out the smoldering wick till he has led the truth to victory: In his name the nations will hope" (Matthew 12:18–21; see Isaiah 42:1–4).

There is another contrast. In the mind of the prophet the return would be a Second Exodus. As in the first, so in the second exodus, God would be leading and accompanying his people. The "joyful messenger proclaims to the towns of Judah, 'Here is your God.'" He is the Lord coming with power. But even the prophet seems to have had intimations that there will be a different kind of Lord, one who will be like "a shepherd feeding his flock, gathering lambs into his arms." For us, he is the Good Shepherd who will gather his lambs into his arms and feed his flock in a way the prophet could not imagine. He is the Son of God who, as Mark tells us, proclaims the Good News and will bring salvation to his people.

But he, too, like the people of Israel, had to make his exodus. The time had come, wrote St. Luke, for him to be taken up (to heaven), and he set his face to Jerusalem (9:51) when he would make his passage, his exodus, from this world to his Father, when he would feed his flock with his own body under the appearances of bread and wine and then live his life to bring reconciliation, peace, and life to them. Of all this John the Baptist was the herald whose unique role was to point to the Lamb of God who takes away the sin of the world (John 1:29). He did that by offering himself in sacrifice from which flows the baptism in water and the Holy Spirit by which we are reconciled, united to him, and through him to his Father.

This ultimately is the consolation, comfort, or strength that the prophet was proclaiming: "Console them....Speak to the heart of Jerusalem and call to her that her time of service is ended, that her skin is atoned for...." But we, too, like the people of old, have to prepare ourselves for the exodus, for the long journey through this world until we meet the Lord. As for them, so for us; the journey may be difficult, we may fall by the wayside, we may be tempted to lose heart, but as the liturgy of Advent and the Scriptures remind us, God is with us: "Here is your God." And he is still with us, in his church, in his word, in his sacraments, in our private prayer from which comes to us strength and consolation: "Blessed be the God and Father of our Lord Jesus Christ who gives us every possible encouragement (consolation); he supports us in very hardship, so that we are able to support others...as the sufferings of Christ overflow into our lives, so too does the encouragement we receive through Christ" (2 Corinthians 1:4,5).

THIRD SUNDAY OF ADVENT

Isaiah 61:1–2a, 10–11
Psalm: Luke 1:46–54
1 Thessalonians 5:16–24
John 1:6–8, 19–28

It is difficult to detect any clear pattern in the texts of today. The first reading from Isaiah 61 is applied to Jesus himself in Luke. The psalm, from the Magnificat, sounds the note of joy that is repeated in the second reading and is found in the first. The gospel is made up of two extracts from John 1 and recounts the testimony of the Baptist. The note of joy is explained by the traditional name attached to this Sunday, Gaudete *Sunday, because we are close to Christmas (see Opening Prayer). But St. Paul is thinking about the second coming of the Lord for which he is preparing the people of Thessalonika. Then again, the first reading and the psalm stress the Lord's coming to the poor, that group who were the special concern of later writers of the Old Testament. The homily that follows is based on the gospel, the first reading, and the psalm.*

There is a good deal about John the Baptist in all four gospels. At first sight this is surprising as he seems to be a transitory figure. Yet on the other hand he had a mission, a mission of some importance that was announced in the Benedictus: "You shall be called a prophet of God, the Most High. You shall go ahead of the Lord, to prepare his ways before him, to make known to his people their salvation." That was his mission. He was the forerunner, the herald of the Messiah who would bring salvation.

As we gather from the gospels, he had a sense of his mission and when he had grown up he retired to the wilderness to prepare himself through an ascetical life, perhaps influenced by the Qumran people of the Dead Sea Scrolls, but also in the tradition of the prophets of whom he was the last. Then suddenly, as it seems to us, he appears to fulfill his mission.

There were certain stirrings among the people and there had been revolts, led by one Theudas and by yet another called Judas the Galilean, who attracted a following, but both had been put to death. There were expectations among the people of the return of Elijah who had gone up with fire, and perhaps would come back with fire. They were, at least some of them, looking for a Messiah who would overturn the Roman power. As the people listened to the reading of the law in their synagogues, they heard of a prophet who would be greater than Moses, and as they sang the psalms they expressed their longing for deliverance: "O shepherd of Israel, hear us...shine forth from your cherubim throne....O Lord, rouse up your might, O Lord come to our help...."

When the Baptist began his mission and the Jewish authorities questioned him, he rejected all their suppositions and those of the people. He was not Elijah come again, he was not a second Moses, he was not the Messiah. He was no more than a witness, indeed no more than a voice crying out, "Prepare the way for the Lord, make a straight path for him." He was not proclaiming the appearance of a great warrior, he was not promising a Messiah who would come with power. His message was a message of repentance, of conversion, of change of mind and heart. His hearers must put down their pride, they must open a way into their hearts, and they must cease from injustice, extortion, and oppression of the poor. He was announcing the arrival of One who would come after him who was more important than himself: "He must increase and I must decrease"; I must fade away, as he did into the prison of Herod. He was foretelling One who would have a greater gift. Instead of a washing with water that was no more than a sign of repentance, the Messiah would bring a richer gift, a baptism that would fill the emptiness of human hearts with the power of God. He would proclaim the Good News to the poor whose hearts were open to the saving word. He would bring healing to the repentant, liberty to captives, and freedom to those in prison. He would bring in a new age of God's favor, his abounding grace that would liberate them from themselves and their sins.

As the liturgy today stresses, that was the kind of Messiah that John was announcing. He will clothe the poor and humble with the garments of saving grace, he will make his people his bride, adorning them with jewels, and they will exult with joy in the Lord. Of all this Mary was the first beneficiary. The Lord looked with favor on the lowly girl of Nazareth and she rejoiced and exulted in him who had done great things for her.

With her we, too, can rejoice, acknowledging the great things the Lord has done for us through his Son, Jesus Christ. But all is not finished. Like the poor ones of the Old Testament, like Mary and Joseph and the other personages of the infancy gospels, we, too, must always have our hearts open to God, waiting for his gracious favors which are offered to us again and again so that we may rejoice and exult in the Lord when we come to meet him.

If the Baptist's mission seemed transitory, he stands ever before us as the witness, pointing always to the Lord who is Savior and the Light that gives life.

FOURTH SUNDAY OF ADVENT

2 Samuel 7:1–5, 8b–11,16
Psalm 88
Romans 16:25–27
Luke 1:26–38

The prophets foretold the Messiah, John the Baptist was his herald, and Mary, the virgin of Nazareth, was his mother. That is what is set before us for our reflection every Advent and all is brought to a climax in the liturgy of today. The "mystery kept secret for endless ages" is now on the point of being revealed with the imminent coming of the Son of God who is to be born of Mary.

But the promise was made long ago and we hear it today through the prophet Nathan's message to David. His offspring will be preserved and God will be a father to him and he a son to the Father: "Your house and your sovereignty will always stand secure and your throne established forever." God is renewing the covenant, made centuries before in the wilderness, and it is now to be invested in the house of David: "I have made a covenant with my servant…and I will keep my love for him always."

In a way that neither David nor Nathan nor anyone else in the Old Testament could have imagined, we find this fulfilled in the highly wrought account of the gospel today. Exploiting numerous texts of the Old Testament, the evangelist tells us that the child to be born of Mary (betrothed to Joseph of the house of David), will be a son of the Most High and that the Lord God will give him the throne of his ancestor David. Then, recalling a passage from the prophet Daniel (7:14), he says that he will rule not only over the house of Jacob but that he will be given rule and honor and worship over all peoples, tongues, and nations and that his reign will have no end. As we read in Matthew (1:21) he will be Savior, Jesus.

Mary, perhaps only partially understanding the tremendous import of the message, wondered in her troubled mind how it could all come about. She is the betrothed of Joseph but not yet married to him. The answer contains the main message of the gospel. She is to be uniquely favored by God; she will be visited by him and as he made himself known on the mountain and in the Temple by cloud and voice, so now "The Holy Spirit will come upon you and the power of the Most High will cover you"; she will conceive by the Holy Spirit "and so the child will be holy and will be called Son of God." To dispel her mental confusion, she is given the sign of Elizabeth. Then comes her all-important consent to the work of God that is to be accomplished in her: "I am the handmaid of the Lord. Let what you have said be done to me," the creative word of God that made her "favored," engraced, and that prepared her for the conception of the Son of God in her womb. By her simple words Mary gave herself totally to the will of God; as it were, dedicated herself to what God was calling her to do. Christian writers, especially St. Bernard, have elaborated on the consent of Mary as a crucial event in the history of salvation. She was not just the physical mother of Jesus. She gave her whole mind and heart and will to the conception of the Son of God, even if she could not foresee all the consequences.

Advent is a time of preparation, a time of waiting, and the Old Testament can be seen massively as a preparation for this culmination of the work of God to save his people. Mary, too, was prepared; she had received a unique grace in what we call, somewhat inadequately, the Immaculate Conception, when God's grace, his "favor," filled her mind and heart. We may like to think that it

27

was in the strength of that grace that she was able to consent with her whole will to the will of God. It was on account of that same grace that she was obedient to the "word." She entrusted herself in faith to God who called her to play her part in his work of salvation.

In all this she is a model for us in our preparation during Advent. As she had faith in God, as she gave herself wholly to him, as she dedicated herself to his purpose and continued to do so until she stood by the cross of her crucified Son, so we must strive always to be faithful, trusting in God who is always faithful to us, even in the greatest difficulties of our life. Through our prayer, through our celebration of the Eucharist, we like her can dedicate or rededicate our lives to God, knowing that he will lead us to the final vision when we shall see him and the son of Mary with his mother.

4

Liturgies of Advent

Year C

Jeremiah 33:14–16
Psalm 24
1 Thessalonians 3:12–4:2
Luke 21:25–28, 34–36

It is a pity that the parable of the fig tree, vv. 29–33, has been omitted from the gospel. It is an image people can easily understand and is part of the message of preparing for the Day of the Lord.

Advent, the coming of the Lord, the coming of the Lord at the end of time, that is what the gospel today is about. Elsewhere we read that the Day of the Lord will come like a thief in the night and that we shall never know the day or the hour. It may seem a little frightening, and the listing of the four last things as death, judgment, hell, and heaven does nothing to allay our fears. The whole matter is somewhat mysterious and we are prompted to ask questions. Why should there be a second coming? Hasn't the Lord Jesus already come? Has he not in his love and mercy lived, suffered, died, and risen again "for us and for our salvation?" If our consciences are clear, can we not pass peacefully from this world when our time comes and we go to meet the Lord? True, we can. What then is all this about the last day and judgment? The trouble underlying this view of things, which most of us share, is that it is too individualistic.

We have to realize in the first place that we are members of the human race, that vast community of human beings whose history reaches back into the mists of time and who will continue into an unpredictable future. All are called, and it is open to all to answer the call of God and live for him—or fail to do so, as most of us have from time to time.

To put the matter as the Scriptures do, God has a plan, a purpose for the whole human race. In Christ he has let us know, at least in part, "the mystery" of his purpose "to bring everything under him as head" and to guide all things and people to the consummation of his saving love when he will appear in glory.

But God's saving purpose has to be worked out in time, through human beings, and only at the end shall we see and understand its whole meaning. Here in this life we are often troubled by the sheer wickedness of this world, the injustices that the powerful impose on the weak, the feverish seeking for wealth, often to the impoverishment of the already poor, the cruelty that some groups and nations inflict on the innocent and the defenseless. There is even the apparent abandonment by God of those who are most in need of his help.

The last judgment means at least this: that when the Son of Man appears with power and great glory, then we shall see that God's purpose has not been frustrated, that in ways hidden from us now, his purpose has been victorious, and that he has been with the poor, the defenseless, and the tortured. In the immortal phrase of Blaise Pascal, "Jesus Christ will be in agony until the end of the world." He is suffering in those who are members of his Body, and at the end we shall all see how he has been supporting them and how, in ways hitherto unknown to us, he has gathered them to himself to be with him forever.

As for us, we are part of the divine plan: "Before the world began God chose us, chose us *in Jesus Christ*" who suffered, died, and rose again for us so that we might be carried over into the kingdom of his marvelous light when we shall see him and his Son in glory with all the saints. The one condition is that we shall have been faithful to him, whatever the sufferings and difficulties we have experienced in this life.

It is for this that we have to prepare not only in Advent but throughout our life. The gospel mentions the more spectacular vices that we must avoid, "debauchery and drunkenness," but also "the cares of life." That seems harsh. The cares of life are so often imposed on us by others. The word "care" no doubt means an undue anxiety about the difficulties of life which may get in the way of our union with God. More positively, St. Paul bids us to seek holiness, that is, "to live the life that God wants us to live," always looking to Christ who gives us his grace so that we may do so. We may then like to make our own the Advent prayer:

Almighty and merciful God,
let neither our daily work nor the cares of this life
prevent us from hastening to meet your Son.
Enlighten us with your wisdom and lead us into his company.[1]

SECOND SUNDAY OF ADVENT

Baruch 5:1–9
Psalm 125
Philippians 1:46, 8–11
Luke 3:1–6

Zion, Jerusalem, these names occur in three successive texts today (entrance, Baruch, the psalm), and we may wonder what relevance they have to Advent. In the Bible, Zion and Jerusalem are usually the same, for on Mount Zion was the Temple, from the time of Solomon the focal point of the life and worship of the people of Israel. There they went up to worship two or three times a year; they looked toward it; they sang about it in their psalms; it was their holy place where God made himself known. It was like a beacon from which the light of God's glory shone out. It was a symbol of the unity of the people of God.

Yet for some it was also a sign of division. The Samaritans would have none of it and had set up their own temple in the northern kingdom. Zion was assailed by enemies, it was laid low, the people were scattered among the nations, and tasted the bitter bread of exile. Today the little-known prophet Baruch, writing, it would seem, from exile in Babylon, predicts the restoration of Jerusalem which he addresses as if it were a person: "Arise, Jerusalem, take off your dress of sorrow and distress" and "put on the diadem of glory of the Eternal on your head." Like other prophets he sees Jerusalem as the bride of God. It will be renewed and restored and made more glorious than it was before. Her people will be gathered from the ends of the earth.

In the New Testament, in the liturgy, Jerusalem-Zion is a symbol of the church, the new Israel of God. For John of Revelation, the church is the new Jerusalem, adorned like a bride to meet the bridegroom. For St. Paul, she is the bride for whom he offered himself in sacrifice that she might be holy and without speck or wrinkle, cleansed in the waters of baptism. In St. Matthew's gospel she is a city set upon a hill and the light of her "good works" must shine out over the world. St. Peter sees her as the ark of salvation.

But also like Zion of old, the church has been devastated by war, reduced by persecution, and her own sons and daughters have obscured the light by their sins. The seamless robe of Christ has been rent by heresies and schisms and they, too, have obscured the light. Like Israel, however, the church has also had her prophets and saints who time and again have called her to repentance and renewal.

John the Baptist, it is true, was addressing a crowd of self-confessed sinners and at a time when Israel was under Roman occupation and, to some extent, divided up among the kinglets he lists. But the church makes his call her own. His message is one of repentance which prepares the way for the renewed coming of the Lord to the church and to us. In our own time, the Second Vatican Council has repeated the *whole* gospel message and called the church to interior and exterior renewal. *Ecclesia semper purificanda, ecclesia semper reformanda*, it declared; the church needs to be constantly purified and renewed if its light is to shine in the world, our world. So the Council at its opening could say that its purposes were to give the Christian people renewed vigor in their life, to adapt the church to the needs of our time and "to strengthen whatever can help to call the whole of humankind into the household of the church" (Constitution on the Sacred Liturgy, I).

But as that same Council has said, we are the church, the people of God, and the message of the Scriptures is addressed to us today. For some, the "changes," the adaptations, have been difficult. So we might like to look at that word "repentance" again. It means a change of *mind* as well as of heart. A voluntary hardening of the mental arteries is not a Christian virtue. Change is a condition of life, and since the church is the body of Christ, change or rather development is an essential feature of its life. Without it the church would be dead, an outmoded sect that would have nothing to say to the world.

Perhaps then, in Advent, when it is customary to have services of penitence, we all might look into our hearts and ask ourselves whether we are hanging on to old ways simply because they are old.

THIRD SUNDAY OF ADVENT

Zephaniah 3:14–18a
Isaiah 12:2–6
Philippians 4:4–7
Luke 3:10–18

Very obviously the note of joy is sounded strongly in the texts of today. It is *Gaudete* Sunday when we rejoice because the feast of Christmas is near. So Zephaniah proclaims, "Shout for joy, daughter of Zion, Israel shout aloud...Exult, [for] the Lord, the king of Israel, is in your midst." His cry is taken up by Isaiah: "People of Zion, sing and shout for joy, for great in your midst is the Holy One of Israel." Then there is the message of St. Paul, "Be joyful, always be joyful in the Lord...the Lord is near."

We may ask: What were the prophets thinking about when they made their exhortations to rejoice? Zephaniah seems to be thinking of the time, now imminent, when the people of Israel will be able to return to Jerusalem. Their liberation is near; their sentence, exile, has been repealed, God has not abandoned them, the Lord is already in their midst, strengthening them and renewing their hope to return to their homeland. He will renew them with his love and—astonishingly—even dance with shouts of joy as on a day of festival.

Isaiah's message seems to be similar. Although it is difficult to date the text, it comes in the context of a passage about the first exodus from Egypt, but there is to be a second exodus from Assyria when "There will be highway for the remnant of his people," for those, still left, from Assyria, as there was for Israel when they came out of Egypt (12:16). The Lord will be in their midst, leading them. The cause of joy for Isaiah also is liberation, deliverance, when the people once more will enjoy freedom and the good things of the promised land. "On that day," and after making their way through the waterless desert, "They will draw water from the wells of salvation."

The prophets' messages, however, were not just for their own time. They are for ours also, and when we hear the word "liberation" we cannot help but rejoice with those peoples who in recent months have been liberated from the tyranny of totalitarian rule and are now rejoicing in a freedom which we hope and pray will not be precarious. But we remember also those other millions who still await liberation in soul and body from the oppression of the mighty in various parts of the world.

But if there is a note of joyful expectation in the Scriptures of today, there is also a message of preparation. As we heard last week, Luke includes Isaiah's verse, "All humankind will see the salvation of God." Today the Baptist is telling his hearers how they must prepare for the coming of the Messiah who will bring a salvation through water and through "the Holy Spirit and fire." That will be the water of salvation, a cleansing baptism, an interior baptism when the Spirit of God will penetrate the human heart. Then it will be a lifegiving water, for "from the heart of Christ will flow fountains of living water" (John 7:38).

For this there must be a preparation of mind and heart and this was very much the theme of John the Baptist's preaching. When various kinds of people came to him asking, "What must we do?" he gave them practical advice suitable to their condition. The notorious tax collectors must take no more than the official rate, not twenty percent more, or thirty percent, or even a hundred percent, as some of them tried to screw out of the people. The soldiers, perhaps Herod's temple police, must not indulge in bullying or extortion; there must be no violence or corruption. They must be content with their pay.

No doubt we are not guilty of such crimes, but the Baptist does suggest that preparation for Christmas ought to have its practical side. The groups of people he was addressing were a pretty earthy lot. They were on the make, they wanted to get as much of everything as they could. We live in a society that puts an inordinate emphasis on wealth and possessions, and we might look into ourselves and ask whether we, too, are not attached to possessions and to worldly values. John's first injunction was "Share what you have with others," and we might consider whether or not we are indifferent to the cries of those still awaiting liberation from the grinding necessities of their situation. The Baptist's statement about a baptism with fire has an element of judgment in it and he speaks of the Lord with the winnowing fan in his hand sorting out the wheat from the chaff. As the evangelist of the fourth gospel says again and again, judgment is now, and he exhorts us to judge ourselves in the present moment in preparation for the judgment that will come at the end of our lives and at the end of time, the final Day of the Lord.

If we do this, we shall be able to welcome Christ when he comes to renew his gracious presence in us on Christmas Day. The forming of judgment, which is a matter of discernment, will be helped if we reflect on the Advent prayer which runs: "Father, you have given us food from heaven. By our sharing in this mystery [of the Eucharist] may we *judge wisely* the things of earth and love the things of heaven."[2]

FOURTH SUNDAY OF ADVENT

Micah 5:1–4a
Psalm 79
Hebrews 10:5–10
Luke 1:39–45

We are on the threshold of Christmas and the longings of the people of old are about to be fulfilled: "O Shepherd of Israel, hear us, shine forth from your cherubim throne. O Lord, rouse up your might, O Lord come to help." Hundreds of years before this was accomplished, the prophet Micah had proclaimed that out of the tiniest clan of Judah would come the shepherd who will feed his flock. Born of a woman of the tribe of Judah, he will rule over the whole of Israel with the power of the Lord. He will bring security and peace to the people for he himself is peace.

Today the promise is kept. Mary, bearing in her womb the desired of the nations, comes to visit Elizabeth, her kinswoman, who exclaims, "How is it that the mother of my Lord should visit me?" As she spoke, the child in her womb "leapt for joy." It may have been a natural occurrence, but she saw it as a sign of the presence of the Lord, though she could not have guessed all that her words implied.

As we ponder on this familiar text we are prompted to ask questions. Did it all happen just like that? Was Mary's action just the kindly visit of one mother to another? Whatever Luke's sources were (and we do not know what they were), he, too, had pondered on the traditions he had received, and he saw in the event something deeper. As he shows in his Annunciation narrative, he knew, he believed that the child Mary was bearing was the Lord, the Son of God, and he turned over in his mind the whole history of God's gracious dealings with the human race. He had thought of the Temple, the place where the Lord made himself present and known to his people, the place called the Holy of Holies, where there was the Mercy Seat overshadowed by the two great cherubim. Perhaps in his mind, too, as in the liturgy today, there were the words of the psalm, "Shine forth from your cherubim throne." He was certainly keenly aware of the importance of the Temple in the infancy story. It was the place of the promise to Zechariah, it was the scene of the Presentation of Jesus, and the infancy gospel closes with Jesus in the Temple. Now the prayer of the psalmist was being answered. Jesus in the temple of his mother was coming first to John the Baptist, his forerunner, who even from his mother's womb was filled with the Holy Spirit (Luke 1:16). He, after Mary, was the first to receive the saving grace of the Redeemer.

For the Temple was also the place of sacrifice and in the Christmas liturgy the conception and birth of Jesus are the beginning of salvation. God would save his people through the body of his Son, the body, the flesh he took from Mary: "You who wanted no sacrifice or oblation, prepared a body for me," and the body formed in the womb of the virgin of Nazareth was to be the instrument of the salvation of the human race. The very body was to be the "sacrament" of his and his Father's will to reconcile the human race: "God, here I am! I am coming to do your will." With a love beyond our imagining the Son embraced his Father's will to save the human race from their age-long alienation from God. Jesus accepted that it was in his body and through the total self-giving of his whole being that he would bring to an end the always inadequate sacrifices of old by the all-sufficient sacrifice he offered on the cross. It was his will that we should be "made holy by the offering of his body made once and for all." It was thus that he brought into existence another Temple which is his own body (John 2:22), of which his mother is the chief member.

If this way of thinking of the Visitation seems a little strange, let us remember that the child Mary carried in her womb and brought forth to the world was the Savior: "My soul glorifies the

Lord and my spirit rejoices in God my Savior," and in Advent we sing of the *Alma Redemptoris Mater*, the dear mother of the Redeemer. She is the "gate of heaven" through whom the Savior came, and she reversed the name of Eva by accepting from the Angel his *Ave* and submitting her will to the Lord's.

About all this we can think as we pray the Opening Prayer of today, in which is summed up the whole work of redemption:

> *Lord, fill our hearts with your love,*
> *and as you revealed to us by an angel*
> *the coming of your Son as man,*
> *lead us through his suffering and death*
> *to the glory of his resurrection....*

Notes

1. *Divine Office* I, p. 5.
2. Prayer after Communion, II Advent.

5

Christmas

ORIGINS

The origins of the feasts of Christmas are different, though liturgically related, from those of the Epiphany which are obscure. So they must be taken separately.

As has been mentioned above, the feast of Christmas is first recorded in a calendar of the mid-fourth century, but there remains the question how it came to be. The most probable view is that it was the Christianization of a pagan festival, *natale solis invicti*, the birthday of the unconquered sun god. The Roman emperor Aurelian had established the festival precisely on December 25 in the third century in the hope of giving a point of unity to the Empire. Sun worship was strong in the East. It was of course associated with certain rituals and was a sign of resistance to the Christian faith. When in 313 the church gained its freedom under Constantine, who was then not a Christian, there was a further development. He, too, honored the sun god (and his portraits suggest that he *was* the sun god), and in 321 he decreed that the first day of the week, Sunday, should be a holiday. A little later in 330 he made possible the building of the basilica of St. Peter on the Vatican hill; and this was about the time the birthday of the Lord began to be celebrated. It was in that place that the Romans had venerated the *Sol Invictus* and Constantine, with his syncretizing tendencies, would no doubt not have been displeased to see the two cults apparently converging. The old one proved to be difficult to eradicate. Even a century later, in the time of St. Leo the Great, people were ascending the hill and bowing to the rising sun.

The content of the Christian feast was, however, very different from that of the pagan feast. Christians had long been familiar with the notion that Christ is the sun of saving justice and often they had heard of him as the light of the world, the light of the human race (John 1:4, 8:12). In a third-century catacomb there is a wall painting of Christ as the sun coming forth like a bridegroom from his tent, the womb of the Blessed Virgin Mary. It was an early interpretation of a text, Psalm 18 (19): 6, 7, which has long had a place in the Christmas liturgy.[1]

There were other influences. In 315 the Council of Nicaea had defined the second person of the Trinity as being "of the same nature" as the Father, equal in all respects to him. Light of Light, true God of true God, who yet came forth from the Father, took our human nature and "set up his tent" among us (John 1:14). This event is thought to have concentrated people's minds on Christ as the Word of God who became a man for us.

As we have seen, the celebration took place in St. Peter's but another council, that of Ephesus (431) coincided with the building of the basilica of St. Mary Major, and that council had defined her as *theotokos*, the mother of God. The celebration was then transferred there. It is not without interest that the words *gloriosae semper Virginis Mariae Genetricis Dei et Domini nostri Jesus Christi"*(the glorious ever-virgin Mary, mother of God, our Lord Jesus Christ) may well have been inserted into the Roman Canon, still in formation, about this time. It is an early witness to the devotion of the Roman church to Mary, the mother of God.

As the calendar referred to above shows, Christmas was first celebrated as a past historical event. It was in a list of the anniversaries of certain bishops and martyrs. But no doubt under the influences already mentioned, the Christian mind pondering on the events and the data of holy Scriptures saw in the festival something more than a mere commemoration. It was a celebration of the mystery of salvation that began with the Son of God taking our human nature as much as the extension of the Paschal Mystery that was celebrated at Easter. This understanding is very prominent in the Christmas sermons of St. Leo that he preached to the people of Rome from about 440 to 450. His understanding of the matter was profound. For him, and for the people who listened to him, the birth of Christ was much more than a remembrance of what had once happened. As he said in one sermon, "It is thus that we can perceive the birth of the Lord *as present* and not simply as a past event which we recall. The proclamation of the angel of the Lord to the shepherds keeping watch over their flocks has filled our ears also...it is as if on this feast it was said once more: 'Behold, I bring you good news of great joy which will come to all the people; for you today is born this day in the city of David a Savior who is Christ the Lord.'" Elsewhere he sees the Christmas event in the perspective of the economy of salvation: "The whole assembly of the people who have come forth from the baptismal font and have been crucified with Christ in his passion, raised to life in his resurrection and set at the right hand of God in his ascension, are born with him in his birth which we celebrate today." Through the celebration of the Christmas liturgy we are (or can be) renewed, reborn, by the birth of the child of the Father who makes himself present to us in the Christmas festival. For Leo, Christmas was the beginning of salvation: "According to God's plan of salvation the sin of the world must be destroyed by the *birth* and passion of Jesus Christ and its effects flow to every succeeding generation." This is echoed in the Divine Office of Christmas Eve: "Tomorrow the sin of the world will be destroyed," and "Lift up your heads, your redemption is at hand." All this is the essential message of Christmas, and that is why it is inseparably linked to the Paschal Mystery of Easter time.

I fear we must put aside the pious elaboration of the meaning of the Three Masses at Christmas: the "birth" of the Word from the Father before time began, his birth at Bethlehem, and his "birth" in the human soul. This was thought up when people did not know how it came to be that there were three Masses at this time. At first in the fourth century there was but one Mass in St. Peter's at about 9:00 A.M. Later in the fifth century after the basilica of St. Mary Major was erected, there was a celebration of the Night Office (Matins) before the Mass and followed by Lauds (Morning Prayer) about dawn. A little later the pope went to the church of St. Anastasia, an Eastern saint, as a compliment to the Greek community and the Emperor, still the official ruler of the whole Empire. Then came the third Mass at St. Peter's. The pope must have been very tired!

It is to be observed, however, that there was only one Mass in each church. It was regarded as an anomaly at the time that there should be more than one Mass in a single church on one day. Like Byzantine Christians to this day, people in the fifth century and later thought that an alternative should be "fasting." Only in very exceptional circumstances could a second Mass be celebrated on the same altar in the same church. But, as with some other papal practices, when the Roman rite was extended to the whole of Europe the custom grew of each priest celebrating three Masses on Christmas Day. That is how it came to be that in parish churches with several priests the whole morning was filled with back-to-back celebrations. Pastorally speaking it was unfortunate. Usually there was no homily and people flowed in and out of church catching the end of one Mass and the beginning of another. It was the result of a misunderstanding of the tradition, and one can only hope that the practice has ceased.

A more recent practice is that the Midnight Mass is celebrated rather earlier, and it is interesting to note that the Roman Missal of 1970, as that of 1570, has the term *Ad Missam in Nocte*, Mass at Night, and in the northern hemisphere "night" officially begins about 9:00 P.M. The reasons for this apparent anticipation are pastoral. People in many places are reluctant to go out late at night and return home in the early hours. The dangers are known to all and priests have thought it better and safer to have the *Missa in Nocte* at a rather earlier hour, though it would seem to be undesirable and an abuse to have the celebration earlier than 9:00 P.M.

MASS OF THE VIGIL

Isaiah 62:1–5
Psalm 88
Acts of the Apostles 13:16–17, 22–25
Matthew 1:1–25

This Mass is to be celebrated in the late afternoon, if possible, in connection with the First Vespers of Christmas.

One thing that strikes us as we listen to the texts of today is that it is an elaborate recalling of the history of salvation, that is of God's saving purpose for the human race. It reaches from the time of the patriarchs (second reading and the gospel) to the promise of the liberation of the people of Israel (first reading), and finally to the coming of the Emmanuel (gospel). But the heart of the saving purpose was covenant, the covenant that God made with his people, and that he renewed again and again even when they had broken it. After various twists and turns of fortune, God made the covenant with David with the promise that the Messiah would come from his descendants: "I have made a covenant with my chosen one, I have sworn to David my servant: I will establish your dynasty forever....I will keep my love for him always; for him my covenant will endure." The covenant, so often broken by the people of Israel in the past, is now going to be renewed in a way no one could have imagined. Joseph and Mary were of the Davidic line and from that line Jesus takes our human nature. He himself is the new covenant; he is the salvation that Simeon looked upon as he held him in his arms; he is love, now incarnate, the love the Father had offered the people throughout the ages.

The prophet had a glimpse, and perhaps more than a glimpse, of this truth when he proclaimed that the scattered people of Israel would be gathered together again into their own land to be one people. They will be given a new name; they will be a crown of splendor in the hand of God. No longer will they bear a name like "forsaken" or "abandoned." They will be the delight of God, they will be his wedded people, they will be his bride. Exaggerated language? No, for the essence of the covenant was love, best perhaps called a love pact, a marriage between God and his people, as so many other texts of the Bible tell us.

What the prophet glimpsed is fulfilled in the conception and birth of Jesus and thus we are introduced to one of the profoundest truths of the New Testament. Early on the church saw the union of the Son of God with our human nature as the marriage of God with his people. The womb of Mary was the *thalamus* (Psalm 18), the marriage bed where the Son united human nature to himself and entered into a marriage with the human race. He made our lowly human flesh his own so that we could enter into a union with him we find difficult to describe. But it is not a baseless imagination. For the Baptist, Jesus was the bridegroom, and for St. Paul, pondering on the Body of Christ, the whole people of God is the bride of Christ: "This is a great mystery—I mean in reference to Christ and his church" (Ephesians 5:32).

It is to this point that the simple narrative of the gospel takes us. But that is not the whole story. The Emmanuel being carried in the womb of Mary will be called Jesus "because he is the one who is to save his people from their sins." The incarnation is the beginning of our salvation and is already effective. "Tomorrow there will be an end to the sin of the world and the Savior of the world will be our King," and we greet him with Alleluias. As the liturgy, as so many carols, have it, the birth leads on to the suffering, the death, and the resurrection, for Jesus is himself the covenant who can make the whole human race one if people will accept his love: "This cup *is* the new covenant in my blood which will be poured out for you" (Luke 22:20). Through the Christmas liturgy, through union with God-the-Son-made-Man, we enter more deeply into that marriage union with him and so prepare ourselves for our final meeting with him: "God our Father, every year we rejoice as we look forward to this feast of our salvation. May we welcome Christ as our Redeemer, and meet him with confidence when he comes as our judge."

Mass at Night

Isaiah 9:1–7
Psalm 95
Titus 2:11–14
Luke 2:1–14

Few occasions in the year are so difficult to preach on as this one. The Scriptures are very rich in content and yet the preacher wishes to be simple, to deliver a message that goes home to his listeners. The Scriptures suggest many themes but all the preacher can do is select one that is central. What follows is an attempt to follow one line of thought.

Deliverance, light, and peace. In these three words the message of Christmas can be summed up. On a people that walked in darkness there shone a great light. A people that lived in the gloom of exile were brought back to their own homes and their hearts are gladdened by the warmth of the reception from their own kind. Their hearts rejoice, for after the wretchedness of war and exile there will be peace, a new kind of peace. This peace will come with the royal child who will be wise like Solomon, courageous like David, but more than that a Prince of Peace, because he will reign with justice and integrity.

All this seems, and perhaps seemed at the time, too good to be true. And yet, and yet, as we turn to the gospel we find that the prophecy has been magnificently fulfilled: "I bring you news of great joy, a joy to be shared by the whole people. Today in the town of David a Savior has been born to you; he is Christ the Lord." The Good News of salvation is proclaimed, the One "who will save the people from their sins" is here and he is nothing less than the royal child. He is the promised Messiah (the Christ) and unimaginably he is Lord, the Lord of heaven and earth, who has come forth from his Father to be with the children of men. Though a child lying in a manger he is king, and to greet him a great light shines in the heavens and the shepherds hear a song that comes from beyond the earth: "Glory to God in the highest heaven and peace for those he favors."

He is Lord, but he is also Savior and the first sign of his saving power is the coming of the shepherds. For these were not the nice romantic creatures of the Christmas card. Perhaps on account of the nature of their work, they were despised by the stricter Jew. They did not observe the Law, they did not worship in the synagogue, they were rough, they had to keep off wolves and other marauders, they had not too good a reputation. Yet they were open to God; they heard the mysterious message and they went to see the child with Mary and Joseph. They became the first witnesses of him who was Savior.

St. Luke thus delicately suggests that Jesus had come to save the people from their sins, to rescue the poor and the outcast, to shed the light of his truth into their minds and to draw them out of darkness into the kingdom that was now beginning. This is underlined by the Letter to Titus. God's grace, God's love, is revealed in the child who is lying in the manger, and this is to tell us that he "has made possible the salvation of the whole human race." This outpouring of God's love toward us demands a response. For his Son we must renounce worldly ambitions, all that leads us from God, and practice self-restraint. If that seems a harsh message for Christmas night, let us say that the word of God is inviting us to put God first in our lives, to be aware of him, and to reverence him in worship and by our daily conduct. This is possible, says St. Paul, because Christ Jesus offered himself, gave himself, so that we could be delivered from wickedness and "have no ambition except to do good"—to help all those who are marginalized, the outcast, the oppressed, those who have nothing, not even a roof over their heads on this Christmas night. The very poverty of Christ should draw us to those who, like him, are poor.

All this—and it may seem much—is the program of the Christian way of living while we are waiting for the second appearance in "glory of our great God and Savior Christ Jesus" who will fill us with his blessings and make us indeed and in truth the people he has called to be his own. The birth of Jesus was the beginning of his great work of salvation, and it can be for us the beginning of a new life in him and for him.

MASS AT DAWN

Isaiah 62:11–12
Psalm 96
Titus 3:4–7
Luke 2:15–20

After the resounding splendors of the Night Mass, this one seems quiet, contemplative, and this is suggested by a phrase in the gospel. True, the shepherds are there and they may have been not at all silent. They witness the event, the baby lying in the manger, and as they went away they told everybody what they had seen, "glorifying and praising God." Nonetheless, that phrase we carry away with us is this: "As for Mary, she treasured all these things and pondered them in her heart." We are invited to do likewise.

The shepherds came, they looked, and went away. Mary in the stillness of her heart pondered on the meaning of the event. It would probably be vain to speculate on what her thoughts were. Luke may well have meant that this was beginning a lifetime's contemplation, for he repeats the phrase in 2:51 after Jesus had come back from the Temple and lived with them. From St. John we know that at the end of this life of him she had borne in her womb she was with him, looking on him now racked with pain on the cross. Such was her witness, the witness of presence.

But as the meaning of this event, which was also a "word," is unfolded to us throughout the pages of the New Testament, we come to know something of its depth and breadth. Today we are led to this understanding as we hear the words, "The kindness and love of God our Savior was shown to us," appeared to us in the child who lay in the manger. God's love for us, *philanthropia*, is present among us so that through the human nature, his very flesh that he took from Mary, he could unite us to his divine nature. As the writers of the first centuries of the church repeated again and again, the Son of God became a man for us so that we might be deified, made children of God, sharing his divine nature.

As the letter to Titus goes on, all this was sheer gift, the pure bounty of compassion for a human race alienated from God by sin. When we hear the words "God loves us" or those other words "God is love," they seem vague and general. They make little impact. St. John was aware of this: "This is the love I mean:...God's love for us [shown] when he sent his Son to expiate our sins" (1 John 4:10). The child of Bethlehem *is* that love, visible, approachable, touchable, present among us, the sign, the sacrament of the measureless generosity of the love that streams out to us from the heart of God.

It is still present among us. He, the Son of God, "generously pours over us the Holy Spirit" so that through his birth we might be reborn, as we were in the waters of baptism, as we can continue to be through the celebration of the Christmas feast, through prayer, through our daily living. Through the Eucharist, through the other sacraments, through the liturgy, Jesus Christ our Savior reaches out to us here and now, and even if we do not see him with our eyes, yet we can respond to him, returning love for love.

This was the event, the word, that Mary pondered on in her heart and like her and with her we can sing: "My soul glorifies the Lord, my spirit rejoices in God, my Savior."

MASS DURING THE DAY

Isaiah 52:7–10
Psalm 97
Hebrews 1:1-6
John 1:1–18

The readings of this Mass are almost certainly the same as those used in Rome in the fifth century when there was but one Christmas Mass. This is not just a piece of useless erudition. It shows us that the Roman church was consciously celebrating the whole mystery of Christ. Hebrews 1:1–6 and John 1:1–14 are indeed not readily understood. But they are proclaiming at once the mystery of God and the mystery of the incar-

nation, and these inevitably go beyond our grasp. We are invited to reflect on them.

The readings of today are like a royal proclamation. There is the herald proclaiming the arrival, the "epiphany" of the great king who is to supersede all earthly kings: "How beautiful are the feet of one who brings good news." And who is coming? "Your God is king," and he is bringing salvation to Israel now returning from captivity but he is also bringing salvation to the whole world: "All the ends of the earth will see the salvation of our God." This inevitably reminds us of the proclamation in St. Luke: "I bring you news of great joy, a joy to be shared by the whole people. Today in the town of David a Savior has been born to you; he is Christ the Lord." He is a divine person, bearing the ancient name of God, Yahweh.

The theme is continued in the psalmist's "enthronement" song. The Lord who is King is coming among his people: "Sing psalms to the Lord with the harp, with the sound of music. With trumpet and sound of the horn acclaim the King, the Lord." And with the psalmist we sing: "All the ends of the earth *have seen* the salvation of our God."

In utterly unpredictable fashion the hope of the writers of the Old Testament has been fulfilled. All through the centuries God has spoken to his people in different ways and through various prophets, but now at last he has spoken to us through his Son, the Son who is the radiance of God's glory and the perfect image of his being. He is Emmanuel, God-with-us.

In his own way, John takes up the story: "In the beginning— before all time—was the Word, the Word was with God and the Word was God." Like God in all things, equal in majesty and power with him the Creator of the universe, he has emptied himself of his glory, he has lowered himself and become one of us: "The word was made flesh and lived among us," as he still does.

So from the depths of God which are hidden from us there now comes the Word who is the revelation of God's love toward us and more than a revelation, for we have the assurance that that love is among us, available to us through the incarnate love lying in the manger. The wonder of Christmas is that the all-holy, all-powerful God who may seem to be a remote and incomprehensible mystery, is with immeasurable generosity turned toward us, is concerned for us, and has for all an everlasting love with which he has loved us from the beginning of the world.

But the coming of the Son of God among us was not just a past event for which we praise and thank God. He came to bring light and life to us, light to dissipate the darkness of our minds so that we can believe, and life so that we can live or try to live "the same kind of life as Christ lived" (1 John 2:6). His work continues among us, for all who accept him in faith receive the "power to become children of God." Jesus is present in his church, he is present in his sacraments, and by baptism we are made children of God. What is implicit in the Night Mass is here made explicit. The consequence for us is that Christmas should be seen as the renewal of our relationship with God as his children. St. Leo the Great expressed this magnificently again and again in his Christmas sermons: "The whole assembly of the people have come forth from the baptismal font and have been crucified with Christ in his passion, raised to life in his resurrection, and set at the right hand of God in his ascension and are born (*congeniti*) in his birth which we celebrate today" (*De nativitate*, VI). It is in this that our dignity as Christians consists, so he exhorts his hearers: "Christians, I beg you, be aware of your dignity and since you have been made sharers in the divine nature do not return to your former baseness by an unworthy life. Call to mind the Head, think of the Body of which you are a member....By the sacrament of baptism you have been made a temple of the Holy Spirit. Do not by wicked deeds make yourself once again the slave of the devil. For you were bought at the price of the blood of Christ and he who has redeemed you will one day judge you in truth" (*De Nativitate*, I).

Note
1. In the Latin psalter "tent" was translated *thalamum*, the bridal bed, which no doubt prompted the interpretation.

6

The Holy Family

Sirach 3:2–6, 12–14
Psalm 12
Colossians 3:12–21
Matthew 2:13–15, 19–23

This feast was included in the general Roman Calendar only in 1920,
and then it was observed on the Sunday within the Octave of Epiphany.
The Calendar of 1969 moved it to the Sunday within the Octave of
Christmas and has added Luke 2:22–40 for Year B, the Presentation of
the Lord in the Temple (thus making it a duplicate of that feast of 2 Feb-
ruary), and Luke 2:41–52, Jesus in the Temple, for Year C, to Matthew
2:13–15, 19–23, the Flight into Egypt). The gospel of the massacre of the
Holy Innocents is reserved for that feast. The new material gives the
homilist an opportunity to preach about different aspects of the hidden
life of Jesus but it must be admitted that the feast still provides problems
for the homilist. It would seem to be one occasion in the year when a
married man or woman should be allowed to preach the homily! The
homily that follows is based on the text of Year A.

As everyone knows (though not everyone is willing to admit it)
family life is not always sweetness and light. When children are
young there is all the burden of looking after them which is a full-
time job that falls for the most part on the mother. Then, as they

grow up and approach adulthood, there are tensions between children and parents. Increasingly, young adults belong to a world that is not that of their parents. The generation gap begins very early! Then the children marry and leave home and establish their own which may be far away from that of their parents. We have been used to the "nuclear" family for long enough, and the old extended family when grandparents, aunts and uncles, and even cousins who could take a hand in bringing up the family, has largely disappeared. There are many other factors in our society that tend to weaken family life and there seems little that we as individuals can do about them. But the problems do not concern only individuals. Their solution lies with the whole Christian community which should be conscious that its task is to foster and support family life in whatever way is possible. Today the Scriptures put before us a whole program that suggests ways whereby we can do that.

The Wise Man of the Old Testament, even though his recommendations are conditioned by a sociological situation very different from our own, emphasizes the duties of children toward their parents. His words are like an extended commentary on the injunction "Honor your father and your mother" (Exodus 20:12). His message can be summed up in three words: respect, honor, and what may be less obvious, service. That last word gives us a useful clue to the meaning of the first two. Honor and respect are shown by action, especially when parents grow old and need affection and help. "Support your father in his old age," says the Scripture, and we would add "support your mother also." Since she often lives longer than her husband she has special need of care. That care is particularly difficult when parents' minds "should fail," and then we are told that we should show them sympathy and we can add, with St. Paul, patience. How such care is to be shown is a matter for families to decide. Modern house design does not make it easy to have aging parents living in the home and often they themselves do not want to do so. Their way of life is and must be different from that of younger people. So it is incumbent on the children, with the full agreement of their parents, to see that they are safely and comfortably housed in what is now called "protected accommodation." But that does not end one's obligations. Constant visits and attention to their emotional and spiritual needs are necessary. I wonder how many remember that their mother prayed with them when they were very young and how aging parents whose minds are wandering may like to be prayed with from time to time.

The Wise Man's advice seems not to go beyond moralizing. St. Paul raises the whole matter to a Christian level. No doubt he was using here and elsewhere in his Letters what has been called the "household code" that was current at the time. But decisively he centers all his advice on Jesus Christ. There must indeed be present in family life the virtues of compassion, kindness, gentleness, and the rest but, as he says, all these are held together by love, the love of God that is implanted in our hearts by the Holy Spirit and which must flow out from us in service to those to whom we owe our existence. Furthermore, the service we give or try to give is sustained by that same love. It can be said, and surely with truth, that love, the love that brings peace and harmony, is the very heart of family life. No doubt that sets an ideal but without ideals we cannot live a life that is worth having.

Then he turns to the relationship between husband and wife. The injunction to wives to "give way," to be submissive to their husbands, may seem to us quite out of date, and we must understand that St. Paul had in mind the conditions of his own time. If we look a little deeper, we find that both husbands and wives must be submissive to the Lord, and the husband is enjoined to *love* his wife, as if it were necessary to remind him of this fundamental quality of marriage. Love rules all as it does in the relationship of children to parents who are bidden to be obedient to them. A difficult virtue at any time and especially when the children are growing up and becoming young adults. They may wish to go their own way, they may insist on going their own way, to the worry and dismay of their parents. Then, above all, parents can "hold" their children only by "the cords of love," a love that is patient, a love that is forgiving, a love that endures and never gives up hope. For "to drive children to resentment" dries up the source of love on both sides.

The Mass began with the care of children for parents and ends with the care of parents for their children. Joseph takes Mary and the child out of danger over the border where Herod's writ did not run and brings them back safely to the peace of Nazareth. (It must be admitted that the passage from Matthew does not fit in very well with the theme of the feast. For Matthew, Jesus was a second Moses who recapitulated in his own experience that of the Israelites who went down to Egypt and were led back by Moses to the "land flowing with milk and honey." Whatever tradition Matthew was using, that is the basic meaning of the passage as is indicated by the quotation, "I have called my son out of Egypt" [Hosea 2:1].)

Family life is based on the reciprocal relationship of love that changes according to need, and if it is *allowed* to change it becomes ever deeper. Then indeed "the peace of Christ" will reign in the hearts of all.

7

Mary, Mother of God

January 1

Numbers 6:22–27
Psalm 66
Galatians 4:4–7
Luke 2:16–21

This is the oldest feast of Mary in the Roman Calendar. It appeared in the seventh century and coincided with the Octave Day of Christmas and the beginning of the civil year. Its emphasis was changed with the introduction of the Feast of the Circumcision of the Lord that came from Gaul. In 1960 the day was once again called the Octave Day of Christmas, and in 1969 it received the title above. It is, however, a somewhat curious amalgam of texts. The first reading and the gospel (last verse) recall the naming of Jesus, which until 1969 was kept as a separate feast on 2 January. The same verse refers to the circumcision. All this presents some difficulty to the homilist. In what follows I have used mostly the second reading and the gospel.

In the New Testament Mary, the virgin of Nazareth, is inseparably associated with her Son who, as this feast proclaims, is the Son of God. As the Council of Ephesus (431) declared, she is *theokotos*, the mother who brought forth into the world the Son of God. In the same century the Roman church inserted that title, *dei genetrix*, into the Roman Canon. This evokes the infancy gospels of Matthew and Luke: "She has conceived what is in her by the Holy Spirit," and "The Holy Spirit will come upon you and the power of the most high will cover you with its shadow, and so the child will be holy and will be called Son of God." As we learn from Matthew he was called Jesus, Savior, for he had come into the world to save people from their sins.

But the oldest *written* attestation of her role in the saving work of God is in the letter to the Galatians which we read today: "When the appointed time came, God sent his Son, born of a woman...." Like Mary who treasured all the happenings at Bethlehem and "pondered them in her heart," the church reflected and continues to reflect on the content of these messages and sees without hesitation that she is indeed *theokotos*, mother of God. It is on account of this that today we honor and venerate and pray to her. As the liturgy, as the poets through the ages have borne witness, she is unique. There is no one like her. She is "our tainted nature's solitary boast."

But that is not all. St. Paul continues: "God sent his Son...born a subject of the Law, to *redeem* the subjects of the Law...." With her Yes at the Annunciation she had given her consent to the divine "word" and she brought forth Jesus who is the Savior of the world. Mother of the Son of God, mother of the Savior by bringing him forth into the world, she had part in his saving mission. We may add that by the upbringing she gave him, by her prayers that no doubt accompanied him throughout his public life, and by her presence at the foot of the cross, she continued her consent to be the handmaid of the Lord who was saving the world. She continues her prayers for the church that is his Body: "God our Father, through St. Mary, Virgin and Mother, you gave us a Savior. Grant that we may experience the power of her intercession as she prays to your Son, who is the Author of Life, Jesus Christ..." (Opening Prayer).

St. Paul, however, did not see the events of Bethlehem and Calvary as the end. "God sent his Son...to redeem the subjects of the Law and to enable us to be adopted as his sons." If we are redeemed, saved, reconciled, it is so that we may be sons, children of God, through the Son who took his human nature from Mary so that we might be like him, bearing his image. As we bear the image of the Heavenly Man, so God looks on us with favor as he looked on the Son of Man when he was here on earth. Of all the children of God, Mary is the first. She first profited from the saving love of God that flooded her being from the first moment of her existence and enabled *her* to give herself totally to his will: "Let it be to me according to your word." As St. Augustine and St. Leo said, she conceived the Son first in her heart and then in her body, but through the body she gave him she established a unique relationship with him. By her faith in God, by her love for her Son, there was formed an even deeper relationship. She was the Bridal Church "without spot or wrinkle," and that is why she can be called mother of the church, mother of all those who by faith and love and obedience are members of the Body, brothers and sisters of Jesus Christ, and children of God. She is the model of the church and we can strive to be like her in faith and love so that the saving love of her Son may enter ever more deeply into our hearts and lives.

As we pray after communion: "Father, as we proclaim the Virgin Mary to be mother of Christ and mother of the church, may our communion with her Son bring us to salvation."

8

The Second Sunday
after Christmas

Sirach 24:1–2, 8–12
Psalm 147
Ephesians 1:3–6, 15–18
John 1:1–18

This Sunday does not occur every year. When it does, it offers us an opportunity to meditate on the mystery of the Incarnation.

The strange and highly poetic language of the reading from Ecclesiasticus may well seem difficult to understand. We ask: What or who is this Wisdom? In the Old Testament it has several meanings ranging from skill in doing things to prudence in the conduct of our life. Here the writer, with others in the Wisdom literature of the Old Testament, sees it as personified, a personified quality of God. It "belongs" to God, or rather it is a partial revelation of God. Created by him, yet it existed before time and will exist beyond time. This wisdom comes down from God and makes its home in the people of Israel, precisely in Zion, Jerusalem, where the Temple is. It is rooted "in a privileged people."

Yet not all is clear until we see St. John taking over the divine Wisdom and filling it with a new content: "In the beginning was the Word: the Word was with God and the Word was God." The Word, Wisdom, is now a Person "who was born not out of human stock or the urge of the flesh or the will of man but of God himself." He is Son, the only-begotten Son of the Father. He is now visible, knowable, tangible, "What we have seen, what we have touched with our hands," for "The word was made flesh and lived among us, and we saw his glory, the glory that is his as the only Son of the Father, full of grace and truth." So from the heart of God comes his Son who is the Light, the revelation of the Father, so that we can penetrate some little way into the mystery of God. Jesus is life, the life he came to share with us not only by "seeing" him in his earthly life, but the divine life that is his, the life that he communicates to us so that we can live in him and he is us: "I have come that they may have life and have it abundantly" (John 10:10).

So it is that Jesus is the revelation of God, and that is not just a theological statement. He shows us that the all-holy and invisible God who lives "in unapproachable light" is yet the God who is turned toward us. Out of his pure bounty he brought us into existence so that we might share his life and his love: "Before the world was made, he chose us, chose us in Christ, to be holy and spotless, and to live through love in his presence." What St. John revealed to us was that God, out of his immeasurable generosity, brought us into existence and pursued us, so to say, with his love that is ever faithful throughout the vicissitudes of history, so that through his Son, now made one of us, the iniquity of sin could be done away and we could be raised up to share his own life. Thus he made us his adopted children, "but what we are to be in the future has not yet been revealed; all we know is, that when it is revealed we shall be like him because we shall see him as he really is" (1 John 3:2).

That is our unimaginable destiny and it is for us to live according to our dignity as children of God and not as children of the world. Christmas is the renewal of the divine love that made us children of God: "Of his fullness we have all received," not just once and long ago but throughout our lives, and we can do because he gives us "grace upon grace." And the grace is his life, nourished by the holy eucharist: "Anyone who eats my flesh and drinks my blood *has* eternal life" (John 6:54). His grace is light so that we may come to an ever deeper understanding of him and so be drawn ever closer to him by love: "Lord, with faith and joy we celebrate the birthday of your Son. Increase our understanding and love of the riches you have revealed in him, who is Lord for ever and ever" (Prayer after Communion, Dawn Mass of Christmas Day).

9

The Epiphany

ORIGINS

The origins of the Epiphany are complicated and have not yet been fully elucidated and perhaps may never be. As the Greek title of the feast indicates, it came from the Near East. As we have seen, the word *epiphaneia*, which means "manifestation," "appearance," or even "ceremonial arrival," was borrowed from pagan customs. That notion has to be kept in mind in any consideration of the feast.

The first mention of some sort of feast on January 6 is found in second-century Egypt, the country of the great Nile. It was observed by a (heretical) sect, the Gnostics, who rejected the birth of a divine person from a human being and held that the divinity descended on Christ at his baptism. This piece of information is not without its importance—the reference to the baptism—but it cannot be said to be the origin of the Christian feast of Epiphany. There was, however, another pagan feast, kept in parts of Arabia as well as in Egypt, of the god Aion, who was often identified with the lengthening of the days, which in those parts of the world was thought to begin on January 6. In this sense the feast was parallel to the Western feast of the sun god, the *natalis sole invicti*. Epiphany too, then, may have been the Christianization of a pagan feast.

There were also other pagan legends current at the time associated with January 5–6. It was thought that the water of rivers, including the Nile, and springs was changed into wine or that the water would remain pure all through the year. It is possible that these alleged phenomena suggested to the Christians a relationship with the baptism of Christ and the miracle of Cana. Certainly we need some explanation of the association of those two events with the Epiphany. A further explanation would seem to be that in the East, Christians were not so concerned about the precise chronological course of events. They saw the manifestation of Christ in its wholeness, reaching from the birth to the miracle of Cana, a perspective that is not wanting even to our Western liturgy. By the beginning of the fourth century there was in the East on January 6 a feast of the birth of Christ which included the passages of Luke (the birth) and Matthew (the visit of the wise men), as well as the baptism and the wedding feast of Cana, which was regarded as closing the events of the early life of Christ.

During the fourth century the Western feast of Christmas made its way, with some hesitations, to the Eastern churches and was kept on December 25, though their liturgies combined the accounts of the birth and visit of the wise men. The whole complexus of these events was regarded as the manifestation and arrival in the world of the great king who was yet the child of Bethlehem. It would seem that under the impact of the Western feast Epiphany celebrated only the baptism of Christ, and that is how it remains in almost all the Eastern churches to this day. Emphasis is given to this by the blessing of the waters that also takes place. This may be a far-off reminiscence of the Egyptian association of the day with the waters of the Nile, though the content of the observance has been radically changed.

Toward the end of the same century the Western church adopted the feast of the Epiphany. It seems first to have been celebrated in Gaul, Spain (where it was associated with baptism), and in North Africa. In Gaul in the fifth century the visit of the magi, the baptism of Christ, and the miracle of Cana were all included in the celebration. Much is uncertain but it would seem that these three events came to the Roman liturgy from Gaul and they are still elements of the liturgy of the Epiphany. Ultimately, they must have come from the East, but in the Roman tradition the three events were separated. The visit of the magi is kept on January 6, and since the days of St. Leo in the fifth century, Epiphany has been a "missionary" feast, the magi representing the gentiles, the pagans, and the beginning of their conversion. The baptism is observed on the First Sunday of the Year, and the miracle of Cana now only appears on the Second Sunday of Year C. We may regret this sharp division but the liturgy sees them all as the manifestation of Jesus as Lord: "The Lord and ruler is coming, kingship is his, and government and power" (entrance antiphon, Epiphany; see the responsorial psalm).

In any case, the Eastern and older elements are to be found in the Office of the day: "Today the church is united to the heavenly bridegroom, for in the Jordan Christ has washed away our sins; to the royal nuptials the magi come with haste with their gifts and at the wedding feast water is changed into wine to the joy of the guests" (antiphon of Lauds). Clearly this text is about Christ's saving work, the effect of which is considered to be present: the church *is* united to the bridegroom and *now* experiences the joy of the wedding feast. It is this, and the Magnificat antiphon that recalls the three events again, that makes the Epiphany a celebration of the saving mystery of Christ. In the liturgy of word and sacrament Christ makes himself present to us and strengthens the bonds between himself and the church. In the Old Testament the people of Israel are called the bride of God, and now the new people of God are bound to him by the self-giving love of his Son, which was expressed supremely by his sacrifice. This is a theme that underlies the whole of the Christmas liturgy.

THE LITURGY

Isaiah 60:1–6
Psalm 71
Ephesians 3:2–3a, 5–6
Matthew 2:1–12

The liturgy today is radiant with light: "Arise, shine out Jerusalem, your light has come, the glory of the Lord is rising on you." In the Divine Office we sing: "The Lord is king, let earth rejoice...Light shines forth for the just and joy for the upright of heart" (Psalm 96). And there was the star guiding the wise men to the child and his mother at Bethlehem.

For us it is not difficult to know that the light is Christ, "the light that shines in the darkness, a light that darkness could not overpower." Indeed in recent months we have seen that more than half a century of brutal repression has not extinguished the light of Christ in human hearts. There is, however, darkness in the world, our world, which has little excuse for blotting out the light of Christ. What is usually called the West, the industrialized, the "civilized" West, is now a post-Christian society where increasing numbers of people do not know Christ or live as if he did not exist. If Epiphany is a "missionary feast," if this last decade of the twentieth century is to be a decade of evangelization, it would seem that evangelization has to begin or, rather, begin all over again, in this Western world. We hardly know yet how to go about it. No doubt programs will be drawn up and, it is to be hoped, put into operation. Meanwhile, we shall do well to think prayerfully about the whole content of the feast of the Epiphany.

Epiphany is revelation, manifestation, the unveiling of God's saving purpose for the whole human race. As we find in the Preface of the feast: "Today you revealed in Christ your eternal plan of salvation and showed him as the light of all peoples." The Epiphany was universal in its scope, the "plan of salvation...for all the peoples" and of these the wise men were the symbols. As the second reading indicates, Epiphany is the revelation of the mystery, that is the mystery of Christ in the wholeness of his saving work. This is spelled out in the first letter to Timothy which forms one of the canticles of the Divine Office: (Great is the mystery of our religion) "He was made visible in the flesh" (epiphany), "attested by the Spirit" (baptism), "seen by angels" (cf. Matthew 4:11), "proclaimed to the pagans" (in the persons of the magi), "believed in by the world " (the proclamation of the Good News by himself and his apostles, and "taken up in glory" (the

Ascension). The whole of his life and redeeming work is summarized here, and of that work the Epiphany was the beginning. This is also suggested by the ancient antiphon we read in Morning Prayer of the feast, quoted earlier: "Today the church is united to the heavenly bridegroom, for in the Jordan Christ has washed away our sins; to the royal nuptials the magi come in haste with their gifts and at the wedding feast water is changed into wine to the joy of the guests." Baptism, the wedding feast of Cana, the visit of the magi are all signs of the saving work of Christ who begins to unite his bridal church to himself. That is the "mystery," the mystery of salvation, though its depth and breadth will only be fully revealed at the end of time. We come to this mystery by faith, and St. Paul prays again and again that we should come to an ever deeper "knowledge of the mystery" so that, as the Opening Prayer says, we may be led from faith to vision: "Lead us from the faith by which we know you now to the vision of your glory when we shall see you face to face."

That is the faith we are exhorted to have, a faith of deep conviction, a faith in Jesus Christ that is a personal attachment to him, a faith that enables us to bear witness to him and to his presence in this unpromising world. With such a faith we can perhaps bear witness by our words, as and when occasion arises, and show that "the plan of salvation" can give meaning, ultimate meaning, to human life to those, and they seem to be many, who can see no purpose in life and live only for the moment.

But as the Epiphany marked only the beginning of Christ's saving work, so does all missionary effort. The end-purpose is that all who hear the word of God and accept it should be united with Christ through baptism and the eucharist and so be brought to the wedding feast where they, like the magi, can offer not only gifts, not only themselves, but themselves in the self-offering of Christ to the Father through him: "Lord, look with favor on your church's gifts: no longer gold, frankincense and myrrh, but he of whom those offerings were but symbols, Jesus Christ your Son, offered by us and received back as our food" (The Layman's Missal).

10

The Baptism of the Lord

This feast marks the end of the Epiphany season. In its own way it is an "epiphany," a showing forth of God of which the signs are the clouds, the voice, and the appearance of the Holy Spirit. The Second Sunday of Year C completes the whole cycle.

We may wonder why we should keep a feast of the baptism of the Lord. It may seem to us just to be a long past event that has little concern with us now. And why did Jesus think that he should be baptized? After all, he had no need of it.

The reading from Isaiah puts us on the way to an understanding of the event: "Here is my servant whom I uphold, my chosen one in whom my soul delights...." Whoever the prophet thought the servant might be, for us there is no difficulty in identifying him. The gospel, echoing the prophet, tells us that he is the Son, the beloved (the chosen one), and on him the Father's favor rests. He is appointed by God "to open the eyes of the blind, to free captives from prison and those who live in darkness from the dungeon." What is more, he is "covenant," the covenant of the people and "the light of the nations." He is the chosen one, he is the humble and gentle servant "who does not cry aloud," who does not break the crushed reed or quench the wavering flame. As we learn from the same prophet in another passage (53), he is the Redeemer who bore our sufferings, who carried our sorrows, who was pierced for our faults and crushed for our sins, and through his wounds we are healed. He is the servant who offers his life in atonement.

This is the servant, as we know now, who is beginning his work of salvation. He had left his village home and had made his way to the river Jordan where John was baptizing. He mixes with the sinners who were thronging around the Baptist, and this is the first sign that he wished to be with the sinners whom his Father had sent him to save. To show his solidarity with a sinful people, he would be baptized as if he, too, were a sinner and to show them that the Baptist's call to repentance was the first and necessary condition if they were to receive his word, which was a word of life. To the Baptist (and perhaps to Matthew) this seemed all topsy-turvy. Was he not the Messiah who had come into the world not to be saved but to save? The Baptist is disconcerted and at first he refuses to baptize him. But Jesus had come to know that he was called to carry out the purpose of his Father.

Then comes the divine manifestation, the intervention of God, the theophany. The clouds are torn apart, the Voice is heard, and the Holy Spirit in visible form comes down and rests on the chosen servant of the Father. It was at once the divine attestation of Jesus as Messiah and the solemn inauguration of his mission and his redeeming work. The full implications of this dawned on the Baptist a little later. Speaking to his disciples he said, "Look, there is the Lamb of God that takes away the sin of the world" (John 1:29). By that word the Baptist evoked a whole series of images that were well known to the Jews. He suggested to his hearers that Jesus was the paschal lamb that the Israelites prepared and ate the evening before they made their passover, their passage from the slavery of Egypt to the freedom of the wilderness where God would bind them to himself by a covenant which would be sealed by sacrifice. So Jesus *is* the covenant, the suffering servant, and the lamb of sacrifice, who by his life, his passion, death, and resurrection makes it possible for the human race, for us, to pass from the darkness of sin and alienation from God to the light of the kingdom.

The second reason for celebrating the baptism of Jesus is that it marks the beginning of *our* salvation. As the New Testament, as the fathers of the church saw, his baptism was the origin and model of our own. Like him we are washed in water and receive the Spirit and so are initiated into the life of Christ: "Unless a man is born through water and the Holy Spirit, he cannot enter the kingdom of heaven." As some of the fathers put it, by his baptism Jesus consecrated the element of water so that it could become the instrument of the sacrament of baptism when we receive "of his fullness," the light that enables us to accept Christ and the power that enables us to become the children of the Father and members of the church.

The servant is appointed to bring God's saving justice, to share in his holiness, not only to a particular people but to the nations, to the whole world, and St. Gregory of Nazianzen shows that he is keenly aware of the solidarity of the human race who it is God's will should be brought into the kingdom that replaces Paradise: "John baptizes, Jesus comes to him...perhaps to sanctify the Baptist himself, but certainly *to bury the whole of the old Adam in the water*; for as he is spirit and flesh, so he consecrates us by the Spirit and water..." Christ is the New Adam, the head of the body, who as he goes up out of the water *"carries up with himself the world*. He sees the heavens split open which Adam had shut against himself and all his posterity, as were the gates of Paradise by the flaming sword...."[1]

The effects of what Jesus did so long ago reach us now through baptism and through the life of the church which is his body and of which we are members. The "favor" God showed to his Son is ours also. It adopts us into the family of the Father and, with the church today, we pray that as children of God "born of water and the Spirit" we may be ever faithful to our calling (Opening Prayer).

Note
1. See *Divine Office* for the feast, I, pp. 379-380.

11

Candlemas

ORIGINS

The presentation has its origin in Jerusalem. The much-traveled lady Egeria (from the West and probably a nun) was there between the years 381 and 384, and gives a vivid if brief account of the celebration. On the fortieth day after Epiphany the people went to the Anastasis (the church of the resurrection) to celebrate the feast which was observed with "special magnificence"; all was done "with the same solemnity as at the feast of Easter" (*at si per pascha*). The presbyters and the bishop all preached on the gospel Luke 2:22–40 (as now), and then the "mysteries" were celebrated.[1] There is no mention of candles until the next century.

The feast first spread to Syria and then to Constantinople where it was called *Hypapante*, "The *meeting* of our great Savior with Simeon the Just when the latter took him in his arms." The emperor took part in the procession, walking barefoot.[2]

It is not until the seventh century that the feast is recorded in Rome where it was introduced by the Eastern pope Sergius I, who may have had knowledge of it in Antioch where he was born. There was an assembly in the forum and from there pope and people, carrying candles, made their way to the church of St. Mary Major. There was no blessing of candles and the pope and clergy wore black vestments, which in Rome were always a sign of penitence. They may be a relic of an earlier procession that would have been observed to counter a pagan rite, though this is not certain. We may remember that until the reform of 1970 the celebrant wore purple vestments for the procession.

In the Frankish empire, the feast acquired the name of the Purification of the Blessed Virgin Mary, and Greek influences are evident. During the procession certain antiphons, for example the *Adorna thalamum tuum*, were sung in Greek as well as in Latin. These were taken over by Rome. It was not until the tenth century that in Germanic lands there was a blessing of the candles, and this was not adopted in Rome until the twelfth century.

The whole rite was reordered for the missal in 1970. The candles are no longer blessed with five long prayers (which originally were meant to be alternatives!), nor are they distributed during the singing of the *Nunc dimittis*. The emphasis is now on the procession. Wherever possible, the rite is to begin in a building other than the church, the candles are briefly blessed with one prayer and *all* go in procession to the church singing appropriate chants. The Mass begins with the collect or Opening Prayer. The rite is now a re-enactment of the "meeting," the coming of the Savior to the Temple, presented by Joseph and Mary, and welcomed by Simeon.

THE MEANING

It may seem that this celebration is no more than a commemoration of an event in the life of Christ that is presented in the liturgy by action and the word of the Scriptures but no more than that.

The first thing to be noted is that the feast is the conclusion of the Christmas festival.[3] As the celebrant says in his introductory remarks, "Forty days ago we celebrated the joyful Christmas festival..." and in the Opening Prayer of the Mass we recall that Christ the Son of the Father became man for us, and in the Second Reading that he shared our flesh and blood so that by his death he could set free those who live in the fear of death (no doubt, eternal death). The presentation, then, is a celebration of the incarnation, certain consequences of which are spelled out in various texts of the liturgy.

One strand of the Christmas liturgy from Christmas Day

through Epiphany to the baptism of the Lord is *manifestation*, the revelation of the goodness and love of God, shown forth to us in Jesus Christ and now made present among us. So in the feast of the presentation we read, "The Lord will come with mighty power and give light to the eyes of all who serve him" (antiphon before the blessing). He is God's "light of revelation to the nations" (first prayer of blessing), and the *Nunc dimittis* gives the same message. Jesus is Light, the revelation of God, who in spite of our sin has taken the initiative and sent us his Son. He is the revelation of divine love and that love is now incarnate in himself. Enlightened by him, we come to faith in God whose will it is that all should be saved.

The presentation is thus also a feast of salvation: "My eyes have seen the salvation which you have prepared all nations to see," salvation that is extended to the people of Israel, to those like Joseph, Mary, Simeon, and Anna whose minds and hearts were open and who were waiting for "the redemption of Israel." The gentiles also will be enlightened, and through faith in Christ they will know the one true God and his saving mercy. The prophetess Anna praised God, for "the deliverance of Israel" had now come.

This theme is suggestively continued by Luke's account. Joseph and Mary go to the Temple to offer their humble sacrifice, the offerings of the poor. This was an act of worship which would be superseded and transcended by the supreme sacrifice of the cross, of which there are overtones in the later part of Luke's narrative.

Then there is the matter of the Temple which has more than one level of meaning in the liturgy of the day and this brings us to the principal emphasis of the feast.

As we have seen, from the fifth century it was called "the meeting," immediately the meeting of Christ with Simeon in the Temple. But here we move into the world of the Christian "mystery," the mystery of Christ whose saving work is celebrated throughout the liturgy. We are not just commemorating the meeting in the old Temple, we are welcoming Christ into the new temple which is his church. As the entrance antiphon of the Mass suggests, "We welcome your mercy, O God, in the midst of your temple."[4] In the liturgies of both the Eastern and Western churches, and in much of the patristic tradition, the Temple is type or symbol of the church and, what is perhaps confusing to the modern mind, "church" meant the "church," the *qahal*, the assembled people of the Old Testament as well as the church of the New Testament. The sense of the feast, then, is that Christ is *renewing* his presence in the church through which he continues his saving work in space and time. Something of this is to be found in the Opening Prayer of the Mass: "All-powerful, ever-living God, we pray that as your only Son was presented in the temple in flesh and blood like ours, we may be freed from sin and presented with him," and we could add "now and when we meet him in glory." Purification or deliverance from sin is an ongoing process, and this feast is a step toward that final encounter with God who, we pray, will welcome us for the sake of his Son.

There is yet another dimension of the feast that is connected with the former theme. In the antiphon, *Adorna thalamum tuum*, which used to be sung in the procession (and now exists in very abbreviated form in the Office), Mary herself is presented as the new Temple, the bridal room of the Lord: "Adorn thy bridal chamber, O Zion, and welcome Christ the King; salute Mary, the heavenly gate. For she has been made as the throne of the cherubim and she carried the King of glory. A cloud of light is the Virgin who has borne the morning star. Simeon, taking him in his arms, proclaimed to the peoples: 'This is the Lord of life and death and the Savior of the world.'" In this Greek text Mary is "the throne of the cherubim" (cf. Psalm 79) who overshadowed the mercy seat in the Temple. She has replaced the mercy seat, for she is bringing "the Lord of life and death, the Savior of the world." She is the "cloud of light," for she, too, had been overshadowed by the power of the Most High who in the Old Testament made his presence known in the cloud, as on Mount Sinai. In this antiphon Mary is a figure or model of the new temple, the church, and she first is the bridal chamber where the first meeting between the Son of God and the human race took place. Furthermore, she is the mother of the Savior and associates herself with his saving work by presenting him, offering, him, to his Father.[5]

If we may see in the gospel a perhaps concealed reference to the passion and resurrection of Jesus, then we could say that the feast, with its many mentions of salvation, looks to the completion of his saving work. The child is destined for the fall and the rising (resurrection) of many. During his life Jesus was a sign that was rejected by some and accepted by others. As he himself said, he was a cause of division. This was true of both the passion and death, and the resurrection. This at any rate is a view that is suggested by the Byzantine liturgy. Great Vespers ends with this troparion: "Hail, O Theotokos Virgin full of grace: for from thee has shone forth the sun of righteousness, Christ the Lord, giving light to those in darkness. Be glad also, thou righteous Elder [Simeon], for thou hast received in thine arms the Deliverer of our souls, who bestows on us resurrection."[6]

In the light of all the foregoing the feast of the presentation is a celebration of the redeeming work of Jesus who is both Lord and Savior. In its own way it unfolds what is implicit in the Incarnation that we celebrate on Christmas Day.

On occasions such as this the homily has to be short so as not to prolong the service unduly, and this provides a difficulty for the preacher. As we have seen, the content of the liturgy is very rich, and it is impossible to do justice to all of it in one homily. One way of tackling the problem is to draw out the meaning of the liturgical *actions* and to center one's remarks on the procession by extending the introductory remarks. The celebrant is not obliged to use the words printed in the missal. He can use other and similar words. Or after the gospel he can exploit the significance of welcome, of meeting, the meeting with Christ in the eucharist. This is suggested by the concluding words of the introduction: "United by the Spirit, may we now go to the house of God to welcome Christ the Lord. There we shall recognize him in the breaking of bread until he comes again in glory."

Commentary on the Scriptures of the day presents further problems. The reading from Malachi is at first sight not at all clear, but exegetes tell us that the "angel of the covenant" is the Messiah who is to come (and is not to be confused with the "messenger" who in Mark is John the Baptist). As we read elsewhere in the same prophet, the Temple and its worship had been corrupted by an unworthy priesthood, and there would come a day when they and their worship would be purified. Only then would the offering of Judah and Jerusalem be welcomed by the Lord. This could be contrasted with the pure offering of the Christ of the Lord who comes gently, almost silently, though he will have a word of power that challenges and divides.

The reading from Hebrews 2:14–18, as has been said above, firmly links the feast of the presentation with the incarnation and redemption.

Perhaps the difficulty of presenting the content of the readings can be got over by brief pieces of (written) catechesis to be read out before the readings.

For the gospel the preacher has the option of using either the shorter or the longer version. Since the longer one is appointed for the feast of the Holy Family, Year B, he may well opt for the shorter one. If so, he might like to note the opinion of the scholars that the very appealing *Nunc dimittis* is the composition of Luke himself.[7] As in all the infancy gospels, it is unwise to use the gospels in over-literal fashion. St. Luke's concerns are strongly theological. He sees this event as the fulfillment of the messianic promise and the foreshadowing of the "redemption of Israel." This controls his whole narrative.

Notes

1. See *Egeria's Travels*, trans. with notes by John Wilkinson (1971).

2. See *The Church at Prayer*, ed. A.G. Martimort, Eng. trans. IV, pp. 88-90 (1985).

3. In the Byzantine liturgy the feast is regarded as if it were Christmas Day itself. Again and again it is spoken of in the present tense.

4. This antiphon is taken from Psalm 47 (48), and in the Hebrew the meaning is somewhat different. It runs, "We *ponder* on your love...." But the compilers of the liturgy in the Middle Ages were using the Latin psalter, translated from the Greek, and when they used the word *suscepimus*, they meant "welcome" or "receiving." Note that in our present liturgy this antiphon is only sung if there is no previous procession.

5. The version of the *Adorna* in the old missal was a very garbled translation that unfortunately obscured much of its meaning. The Greek is a text of the Byzantine Great Vespers and of course is still used. For the purposes of our rite one would have thought that a new and correct translation could have been made set to an appropriate chant to be sung, perhaps at the end of the procession. The above translation is taken from *The Festal Menaion*, trans. Mother Mary and Archbishop Kallistos Ware, London, 1969.

6. *The Festal Menaion*, pp. 416-417.

7. See *New Jerusalem Bible*, Luke 2:29-32, note K.

12

The Presentation of the Lord

Malachi 3:1–4
Psalm 23
Hebrews 2:14–18
Luke 2:22–40

Although this celebration is very beautiful with its lights and joyful songs and movement, it is important that we should not regard it as so much holy play-acting. We have gathered together today to welcome the Lord Jesus who comes to take possession of the church, that is ourselves. This is made clear by what we do and by what his word and the words of the liturgy tell us.

We carry lighted candles in our hands and, as the song we have sung reminds us, we are, as it were, carrying Christ who is "the light to the nations and the glory of his people Israel." As we are told in the gospel of St. John, he is the light of the world and those who follow him will not walk in darkness but will have the light that gives life. So we have prayed that we who carry the candles may walk in the path of goodness and so come to the light that shines forever.

The candles are symbols of Christ himself, and with Joseph and Mary we have come to present him "in flesh and blood like ours" to his Father. Through him and with him we offer ourselves and our lives to the Father. That is the beginning of the goodness the prayer speaks of. But so that our offering may be acceptable, we have prayed that our hearts may be freed from sin so that we may be made fit to enter at last into the presence of the all-holy God.

For this feast is all about meeting. Jesus is brought to the Temple and there in the person of Simeon he meets those whose hearts were open, those who were waiting for "the deliverance of Israel." Prompted by the Holy Spirit, says the gospel, Simeon welcomes him, takes him in his arms, and recognizes in him the Savior of the people, both Jew and gentile. With prophetic insight, he sees that the child is set for the fall and rise of many. He will be a sign of contradiction and his work and his life, death and resurrection, will divide those who accept him in faith from those who reject him. Even so, Simeon could not know that the body he held would suffer, die, and rise again "to atone for human sins."

Here in this eucharist we are about to celebrate we meet our Savior who makes himself present and available to us, so that through our meeting with him once again we may be renewed in body, mind, and spirit. Through him and with him we offer ourselves to the Father, and we pray that as we meet him in holy communion he will bring to perfection God's graces within us so that we may live for Christ and be prepared to meet him again when he comes to give us a life that is everlasting (Prayer after Communion).